CHINA

THE KINGDOM OF THE DRAGON

BARNES & NOBLE

NEW YORK

1 A COUNTRY MAN IN THE SOUTHERN PROVINCE OF GUIZHOU, WEARING THE TYPICAL HEADDRESS, TRIES HIS PRECIOUS RICE HARVEST.

2-3 THE GREAT WALL UNWINDS AMONG THE SNOW-FLECKED MOUNTAINS OF JINSHANLING IN HEBEI, IN ONE OF ITS MOST SPECTACULAR STRETCHES.

4-5 FROM THE WESTERN FACE OF MOUNT LINGYUN IN SICHUAN PROVINCE, THE INSCRUTABLE GAZE OF MAITREYA, THE BUDDHA OF THE FUTURE, LOOKS OUT INTO INFINITY.

6-7 DURING THE RITUAL CEREMONY OF CIRCUMAMBULATION, A DEVOTEE TURNS ONE OF THE BEAUTIFUL PRAYER WHEELS IN THE SAKYA TIBETAN MONASTERY.

8 IN A FAR-FLUNG CORNER OF SICHUAN, IN THE SOUTH-WEST OF CHINA, ALTHOUGH IT IS RIPPLED BY A LIGHT BREEZE THE SURFACE OF THE RICE FIELDS REFLECTS PEOPLE AND TREES AS THOUGH IT WERE A MIRROR.

9 FROM LEFT KING WU, ONE OF THE FOUNDERS OF THE ZHOU DYNASTY, WAS AN EXAMPLE OF AN IDEAL RULER; A BRIGHTLY COLOURED PAINTED DRAGON IN AN ARTIFICIAL CAVE IN THE TIGER BALM GARDENS IN HONG KONG; AN ARTIST IN THE PEKING OPERA PUTTING ON HIS MAKE-UP.

EDITED BY
MARCO MORETTI

TEXTS BY
GIANNI GUADALUPI
MARCO MORETTI
FEDERICA ROMAGNOLI

EDITORIAL DIRECTOR
VALERIA MANFERTO DE FABIANIS

GRAPHIC DESIGN
CLARA ZANOTTI

EDITORIAL COORDINATION
GIADA FRANCIA
FEDERICA ROMAGNOLI

© 2005 White Star S.p.A.

This 2007 edition published by Barnes & Noble, Inc. by
arrangement with White Star S.p.A.

TRANSLATION: Studio Traduzioni Vecchia, Milan

ISBN-13: 978-1-4351-0033-6
ISBN-10: 1-4351-0033-6

1 3 5 7 9 10 8 6 4 2

Printed and bound in Indonesia

Color separation by Chiaroscuro, Turin

CONTENTS

INTRODUCTION

China has awoken, but contrary to Napoleon's prophesy, the world is not trembling. Today Beijing is invading other continents with goods, not soldiers; it is bringing disciplines and knowledge to our homes that are the product of ancient traditions, the most familiar aspects of a country that is otherwise still largely unknown. Now that China is portrayed daily in the media as the up and coming "elsewhere," as the template of the economy of the future, with growth rates as ceaseless as they are steep, it is easy to forget that China is an ancient, beautiful country with millennia-old traditions, unique monuments and breathtaking landscapes. With Deng Xiaoping's famous motto "It doesn't matter if the cat is white or black, as long as it catches the mouse," after the death of Mao Zedong the country abandoned ideology in favor of pragmatism. The result is that its cities are experiencing something akin to the Japanese boom of the Seventies; but this time, an elementary demographic calculation multiplies the size of the boom by at least ten. But beyond Beijing, Shanghai, Canton, Hong Kong, beyond the tens of metropolises, lies an unknown China. The vast western provinces, through which the Silk Route passed, with tablelands crossed by majestic rivers, and the many ethnic groups who have an almost Indian skin-tone, although they have been an integrated part of China for years: this is an area of strong contrasts, which rises to extraordinary heights with Mt. Everest, the highest mountain in the world, but also plunges into the Tarim Basin, one of the lowest and largest basins in the world. The two main rivers, the Yangtze and Huanghe (Yellow River), which run from west to east, span most of the country. Along them one encounters man-made masterpieces, and incredible natural wonders such as the dreamlike spectacle of the Three Gorges of the Yangtze, which has been lauded by poets throughout the ages. Or, farther north, the matchless Buddhist rock sculpture complexes, and a myriad of other cultural sites in the basin of the Yellow River, where Chinese civilization was born thousands of years ago. Still farther north, the Great Wall, the most famous achievement of China's genius, extends endlessly from to the west. North of it the fields, steppes and deserts of Mongolia open up. These immense stretches of land are dotted with nomadic camps, in a triumph of green and ocher. The commonplace of a China that is uniform in terms of language, race, customs and faith is belied by the cultural richness that its fifty-six minorities express; by the arch-roofed mosques of Xi'an; by the western provinces, and by the religious syncretism which for over a thousand years has seen Taoist, Confucian and various Buddhist doctrines mingle and balance each other. For thousands of years, the endless land of China, as vast as a continent, has been the crossroads for peoples, ideas and religions which came from the Siberian steppes, from Mongolia, from Central Asia, from India and Southeast Asia. In cities such as Hong Kong and Macau, Tianjin or Qingdao, Chinese culture has also had to contend with the Europeans, thus generating remarkable values and lifestyles.

Today, China is racing toward modernity and wealth, but also desires to rediscover her roots in tradition, rites and heritage which the Cultural Revolution attempted to obliterate. These are the key elements needed to understand this country. They are accessible today thanks to the slow transition following the reforms Deng Xiaoping brought about; this transition has led the country toward a new version of Confucian pragmatism in which nationalism joins the free market and respect for hierarchy melds with the dream of mass well-being. In this China, the red flags are increasingly making way for red lanterns; monasteries and temples closed under Maoism are being reopened; historic buildings and palaces inherited from the imperial dynasties have once again become a source of national pride. It is precisely this blend of the ancient and the futuristic – found in cities where sci-fi skylines stand alongside millennial monuments and values that have remained unchanged for centuries – which makes China today a unique, fascinating country; a country that must absolutely not be overlooked, because it is here that the hopes and future of a large part of the human race are being played out. (M.M.)

HISTORY OF THE MIDDLE KINGDOM

22 CLOCKWISE FROM LEFT AND 23 KUBLAI KHAN; LIN BIAO, MAO ZEDONG AND ZHOU ENLAI DURING THE CULTURAL REVOLUTION; YOUNG PEOPLE FROM A COMMUNE IN THE SIXTIES; ON JANUARY 8TH 1841 THE ENGLISH FRIGATE NEMESIS DESTROYED SEVERAL CHINESE JUNKS; RED GUARDS SING THE PRAISES OF MAO, CLUTCHING THE LITTLE RED BOOK.

24 AND 25 FUXI (LEFT), ONE OF THE THREE TRADITIONAL PRE-DYNASTIC SOVEREIGNS, WAS THE MYTHICAL PROGENITOR OF THE CHINESE. THE SHANG DYNASTY, THE FIRST DYNASTY THAT IS NOT ENVELOPED IN THE MISTS OF LEGEND, WAS FOUNDED BY TANG (RIGHT).

THE DAWN OF THE CHINESE WORLD

The origins of the Chinese are remote, very remote indeed. The first Chinese man, called Pangu, appeared between the sky and the earth, separating one from the other, several millions of years ago. Then came the thirteen Emperors of the Sky who reigned for 234,000 years; the eleven Emperors of the Earth, for 198,000 years; and the nine Emperors of Men, 45,000 years. The first had a serpent's body; the second had the face of a maiden, the head of a dragon, the body of a serpent and horse's hooves; the last had the face of a man and a dragon's body. In this first, endless period, the Chinese lived in caves or crouched in trees, like birds in nests, and they rode winged deer and dragons. They dressed in leaves and hides, did not know about fire and were discontented; but their sovereigns had chariots drawn by six unicorns. Thirteen imperial dynasties followed, the last of which was founded over five thousand years ago by Fuxi. He had the body of a dragon and invented writing, marriage, sacrifices for the spirits of the sky and the earth, the calendar, music and laws, having seen them drawn on the back of a dragon-horse that emerged from a lake. His successor, Shennong, on the other hand, invented agriculture, medicine, and markets; but also the first ever war.

Among Shennong's descendents, the Yellow Emperor stands out. Shi Huangdi reigned for one hundred years (from 2699 to 2599). He levelled mountains, opened up roads, minted the first coins, while his wife Luizu taught the people the art of breeding silkworms and weaving their product to make clothes. Under the reign of his successor and son Shaohao, the phoenix appeared in China; this bird does not show itself unless good monarchs are ruling.

And so the legends go. History, however, tells of a first dynasty, known as the Shang or Yin, which dates back to the Bronze Age, around 1500 B.C. During this period, many discoveries were made, including writing, metal-working, the war chariot, and divina-

tion. This last practice is behind the discovery of a large number of bones and tortoiseshells (over a hundred thousand) with inscriptions: they were placed in the flames, and the cracks created by the heat were used to tell fortunes. The result was written on the bones themselves, and then kept in special archives. The discovery of these archives has allowed archaeologists to reconstruct many aspects of the Shang civilization; it was a military monarchy that had thirty rulers, had its center in the Yellow River valley, and organized large-scale war expeditions to procure slaves. War chariots and bronze weapons ensured that the Shang armies gained superiority over neighboring sovereign territories. The Shang state was based on a large number of bureaucratic functionaries; the aristocracy was divided into eight separate classes and the population worked mainly in agriculture, cultivating millet, oats, sorghum and wheat (very little rice), without the help of plows and draught animals, which were only introduced later. Vast forests and marshes still covered most of the country, and were inhabited by many wild animals including elephants and tigers. Religion was basically a cult of fertility: of the fields, domestic animals, and women. Belief in the next world meant that objects used by the deceased when alive were placed in the tomb; and to accompany noblemen into the afterlife, their servants were killed, sometimes in their hundreds. Animals and people were also sacrificed to gain favor with the divinities. Male and female shamans chased evil spirits away, carried out spells, foretold the future and induced the rain to fall from the sky.

The Shang dynasty ended just before 1000 B.C., due to the "iniquity" and "incapacity" of its last representatives, such as Zhouxin, who is described as a cruel monster. But the only historical sources that remain are hostile to him; they praise the revolt against that demoniacal tyrant as if it were a war of liberation desired by the heavens. This cliché, of the perfidious last ruler, is one which repeats itself in Chinese historiography with every change of dynasty.

Founded by Wu, a warrior who vanquished and decapitated Zhouxin, the new dynasty, called the Zhou, lasted for several hundred years, until 221 B.C. according to traditional chronology, which, however, is unreliable. The Zhou state had much in common with the feudal monarchies of medieval Europe. The emperor assigned to members of the ruling family, aristocrats and dignitaries vast areas of land on which they could create wealth from the work of peasants and artisans. In exchange, they had to provide armies to defend the empire, pay taxes and send farmhands to the sovereign's fields. The huge number of feudal domains usually consisted of a city and the surrounding countryside; subsequently, many of them were agglomerated in the hands of a single family, forming principalities that became increasingly powerful and fought each other for hegemony. The warriors fought standing in war chariots that could carry three men in addition to the charioteer; they were armed with arrows, lances and swords made of bronze, which was then replaced with ones made of iron when metal-working and forging techniques improved. Once iron was introduced, the life of the peasants also changed; now they could use tools such as the plow and the hoe, while the invention of harnesses with breast-straps meant that draught animals could be used more efficiently.

The war chariots were replaced by archers and crossbowmen on horseback, and the cities were protected by walls. This occurred because, at the end of the 5th century B.C., the period of the so-called Warring States had commenced: two hundred years of wars among the feudal states, thriving on the break-up of the central power of the Zhou. The man who put an end to this bloody chaos was Prince Zheng of Qin, who later took on the title of Shi Huangdi or August Sovereign, which was then passed on to all the emperors; he unified all the tiny rival Chinese states into a centralized empire, yet strangely ancient historiography portrayed him as a monster in. He is described as a sort of bogeyman with a big nose, huge eyes, and "the voice of a jackal, the heart of a tiger and a wolf." The bastard son of the queen of Qin and one of her ministers, he drove his father to suicide and persecuted his mother before taking power at the age of twenty-five; in just over five years he conquered all the neighboring realms and proclaimed himself Emperor of China. In order to defend he country from the incursions of barbarian tribes from the north, he built the Great Wall (or rather, completed it, linking up the scattered sections that had been built by his predecessors): 1500 miles (2400 km) long, it is the largest structure ever built by man, next to which, said Voltaire, "the pyramids of Egypt are merely piles of useless stones." And the Great Wall was certainly useful, being "the ruin of one generation and the salvation of many." For many centuries, the nomad marauders could not manage to break through it, and once their attempts to conquer the East failed, they turned to the West, destroying the Roman Empire.

Shi Huangdi, the First Emperor, was not only a ruthless conqueror. Once China had been unified under his scepter, he set about ruling the country much better than the previous rulers had done. He stripped the feudal lords of their power, replacing them with functionaries that he nominated himself; he unified the legislation of the various states; coined a single currency; assigned ownership of the land to the peasants; built a road network to link up the more remote parts of the Empire; and transformed the capital Xianyang into a splendid city, forcing the nobility to built magnificent palaces there. Like many other monarchs who have passed from history into legend, it is said that he traveled incognito all over the country, hunting out exploitation and righting misdeeds. He loved scientists, but not men of letters, who in turn were against him, as they believed that a strong central government would limit their freedom. When they suggested that he re-establish feudalism "in order to be consistent with ancient customs," he reacted by ordering that all the books describing such ancient customs be burnt. The only books that escaped the bonfire were scientific texts and the works of the philosopher Mengzi (Mencius); but the imperial library still held copies of the forbidden books, which could be consulted by academics. Many intellectuals who protested were condemned to death, others ended up building the Great Wall. Some scholars hid books (written on strips of bamboo) in the walls of their houses, others learned them by heart. The works of Confucius were saved by commitment to memory, but are also full of mistakes for precisely that reason: memory is not infallible. Having thus freed the present from the ties of the past, and escaped various assassination attempts, Shi Huangdi was convinced he had founded a dynasty that would have ten thousand descendents. It finished, however, with his son, who just had time to build his father's grandiose tomb (rediscovered a few years ago, and only partly excavated) before being killed by the populace in revolt.

There followed a period of unrest and fighting between the various pretenders to the empire. Two great personalities emerged: Xiang Yu and Liu Bang. The former, from a patrician family, was a kind of giant, with a terrifying appearance; he loved wine and women and was a brilliant commander. The latter, the son of peasants, was a modest village gendarme. Their long duel, which ended in 202 B.C. with the defeat and death of Xiang Yu, represented the battle between aristocracy and the masses.

Liu Bang founded a new dynasty which he named the Han dynasty; it continued for four centuries. The greatest of his descendents was Wu, who reigned for half a century, from 140 to 87 B.C. He extended the borders of the empire, annexing Annam, Manchuria and Korea, overturning the policies of his predecessors who had merely defended themselves from attacks by the nomads of the steppes. He also sent several expeditionary corps to Mongolia and Central Asia to fight the Xiongnu, an aggressive Turkic tribal people, wiping them out. Liu Bang's desire for conquest was matched by his desire for the elixir of life and he sent groups of wizards in search of the Islands of the Blessed to obtain it. But the islands were never found. He strengthened the power of the monarchy against centrifugal forces and set up administrative processes for the Chinese state, which, with a few variations, would remain functional for centuries and centuries. In order to prevent a few wealthy people from "having the privilege of the exclusive use of the wealth of the mountains and the seas, earning a fortune and ruining the poor," he established that all natural resources were imperial property: he was in fact a socialist sovereign. The production of salt, iron and alcoholic drinks was declared a state monopoly, and with purchases and sales carried out at the appropriate moment, the government attempted to regulate and stabilize the prices of agricultural commodities. The construction of roads and bridges and the digging of canals helped commerce; the capital Chang'an became the world's most populated city; the subjects paid an annual tax of 5 percent on their income, and thanks to that minimal taxation both individuals and the state prospered. As a result, "wisdom flourished, poetry abounded." This sort of golden age did not last beyond the life of the emperor whose wise reforms had promoted it. Floods and drought took it in turns to afflict the peasants, and in addition to natural disasters there was unrest and rebellion in various provinces. Almost a century passed before another reformer took the throne of China: Wang Mang, founder of

28-29 THE PAINTING SHOWS LIU BANG, WHO WAS TO BECOME THE FIRST EMPEROR OF THE HAN DYNASTY
WITH THE NAME GAOZU, ENTERING THE GUANZHONG REGION DURING THE CAMPAIGN TO CONQUER QIN.

29 LIU BANG, LEFT, WHO WON THE CIVIL WAR, WAS OF PEASANT ORIGINS. HIS DYNASTY, THE HAN, LASTED FOR OVER TWO HUNDRED YEARS. AFTER THE FIFTEEN YEARS OF USURPING BY WANG MANG, LIU XIU, RIGHT, REFORMED THE DYNASTY; FROM THEN ON IT WAS CALLED THE EASTERN HAN, AS THE CAPITAL WAS TRANSFERRED TO THE EAST TO THE CITY OF LUOYANG.

the Xin dynasty, who was, however, its only ruler. He is described as the most perfect example of the Chinese gentleman – although he may have had his predecessor, a child, poisoned in order to take power. He was wealthy but loved the frugal life, scorned petty politicians and was the friend of intellectuals and philosophers; he was also impressed by the vast developments of the landed estates on which slaves were used. He revolutionized society by abolishing both slavery and land ownership, nationalizing the land and dividing it into equal parts among the peasants. It nonetheless appears that this far-reaching renewal of the Chinese social system was implemented in an erratic manner, with continual changes of direction and backtracking that aroused bewilderment and discontent. Yet it was Nature that defeated Wang Mang: there was a series of terrible floods, during one of which the Yellow River even changed its course, moving by several miles. The famines and epidemics that ensued shook the richest and most populous region of the empire. The mass uprisings that the imperial army could not manage to repress were joined by the open revolt of the patrician clans that had been upset by the reforms; at the head of these clans was the Liu family, a secondary branch of the Han dynasty. In 23 A.D. the capital was seized, Wang Mang was killed and Liu Xiu proclaimed himself emperor of the newly risen Han dynasty, known as the Later or Eastern Han dynasty, since the capital was moved east, to Luoyang.

31 From the beginning of the 3rd to the end of the 6th century, China once again broke up into a number of large and small kingdoms that fought each other, while Buddhism took root in the country: having been introduced to China by merchants who travelled all over Asia, first it was taken on by the more educated classes, and it later spread throughout the population, to whom it offered a message of hope during times of crisis. Left, the Emperor Wu of the Southern Liang, ruler from 502 to 549 and a fervent follower of the new religion, has himself tonsured as a monk. Right, a detail from the painting.

The catastrophes, civil wars and invasions of the barbarians from the steppes trying to take advantage of the empire's state of anarchy drove much of the population (then about 21 million) to emigrate southward, beyond the Yangtze. They moved to territories which had recently been annexed and had until then been inhabited by other races, who were pushed toward the more inaccessible mountainous regions; the more appealing areas became Chinese and rice cultivation, the most suitable for those well-watered regions, became vastly widespread. The later Han dynasty lasted just under two centuries and its emperors became increasingly weaker when faced with the excessive power of the feudal lords, while within the court itself the gangs linked to the eunuchs or to the empresses' families prevailed; the bitter power struggles often degenerated into bloody battles, in which entire clans were wiped out. In the year 170 B.C., having exterminated the large patrician families of the Dan and the Chen, the eunuchs turned against the scholarly functionaries. They eradicated them, but were not able to replace them in the administration of the empire, and once more the breaking up of the state provoked a peasants' rebellion. In 184 came the revolt known as that of the Yellow Turbans, after the headdresses of its adherents, who combined religious motivations with social and economic demands. The uprising was crushed by two generals, Dong Zhuo and Cao Cao who, having realized the weakness of the central power under the boy emperor Xian, then started the civil war so as to take control of the throne.

Dong Zhuo was victorious, but was later assassinated, and Cao Cao took over the whole of northern China. But he was not able to control the south, and the empire broke up into different sovereign states, and stayed divided for several centuries: this was the period that western historiographers usually define as the Chinese medieval age, during which feudal structures prevailed again, to the detriment of the central power. Aristocratic clans and barbaric invaders from the North carved up China, founding ephemeral states, which at some points numbered as many as twenty and often lasted just a few decades. Foreign conquerors — Tibetans to the west, Turkic peoples and Protomongols to the north — were nomad shepherds reigning over an agricultural, sedentary Chinese population; but they soon assimilated the superior culture of the vanquished, and subsequently became completely Chinese in their ways.

As in the Europe of the barbarian invasions and monasticism, in China during that long period of uprisings and civil wars there were many people who were disgusted by the world around them and sought refuge in spirituality. There was Taoism, which had transformed itself from a religious doctrine into a religion and a system of magical practices aimed at ensuring immortality, and also the Confucianism of the scholars, based on the cult of ancestors and respect for ancient traditions. These were joined by Buddhism, which was introduced to China in the 1st century A.D. by missionaries from India. This was the first foreign religion to penetrate the country, and in those calamitous times it promised redemption through a series of reincarnations and eventually, final dissolution into Nirvana, the end of all pain linked to existence. The first to convert were the merchants who through their work moved into the steppes of Central Asia and crossed the Himalayas, entering into contact with different, fascinating worlds; then the members of the upper classes were struck by the Buddhist culture, and finally the populace was. They welcomed Buddhist preachers, founded monasteries, translated the sacred texts, and made tiring but exhilarating pilgrimages to the sanctuaries of their new faith. They went along the Silk Route as far as Iran, the Indian peninsular, the island of Ceylon, where the Master left his traces and his relics, which the pious converts purchased for their weight in gold and took back to China after years of pilgrimages over land and sea. As early as the 5th century, Buddhism had become the dominant religion, having penetrated all social strata, from nobles to peasants, from Chinese to foreigners, reaching both the imperial court and the country village.

One century earlier, in about 300, the large capital cities Chang'an and Luoyang had just under two hundred monasteries, large and small, with thousands of monks; social disorder, disasters and wars certainly helped that number to grow. In addition, many desperate people became monks not so much due to a vocation as to their need to find a roof and a bowl of rice.

The crude rulers of the North, who had just exchanged their nomadic tents for palaces, received monks as if they were wizards who had the power to work miracles, possessing particular knowledge of the spells needed to invoke the rain essential to an agrarian civilization. The imperial leadership, which already traditionally had a religious role, took the new faith under its protection and made it into a state church, with a monk-official nominated to lead it. The rulers donated assets and land to the monasteries, financed the translation of the sacred texts, and had colossal monuments built such as the statues of the Buddha carved out of rock faces.

In 581 an aristocratic warrior from the North, Yang Jian, who had a brilliant career as commander behind him, decided it was time to build a united empire once again. He seized power in Chang'an, declared himself the Son of Heaven, and founded the new Sui dynasty. He then made an armistice with the Turkic peoples who were threatening the northern border, so he could dedicate himself to conquering the South without being attacked from behind.

In 589 his armies entered Nanjing: after four hundred years, China was unified once again. But the Sui did not last long: Yang Jian, who was industrious in his anxiousness to reign but morbidly diffident and avaricious, was succeeded by his son Yang Guang in 604. Yang Guang redistributed to the peasants uncultivated land that had been abandoned during the endless wars, restored the Great Wall, and had the huge Imperial Canal dug by a million laborers. However, in order to finance his military campaigns he imposed heavy taxation that alienated him from the aristocracy. Li Yuan, a nobleman from the north, led

33 LEFT Under the Tang dynasty, courtly life was refined and splendid, thanks also to the riches that poured into the empire from all over the world; meanwhile, China exported her own products, especially silk. The courtly lady shown in this painting is dressed in sumptuous silk robes.

33 RIGHT The Sui were replaced by the Tang, under whom China had its most splendid military, economic and cultural period. The greatest sovereign of this dynasty was Taizong (626-649), shown here surrounded by his concubines.

a rebellion that ended with the flight and assassination of Yang Guang, and in 618 Li Yuan assumed the imperial crown. Under Li Yuan's dynasty, the Tang, China became the greatest and most civilized power in the world. This was thanks to great rulers such as Taizong (626-649). He took the throne at the age of twenty-one and inaugurated his reign by killing all his brothers, who were competing with him for power. He then began a series of campaigns to crush neighboring populations; his vanguard reached Afghanistan, and Sassanid Persia asked him for help when under attack by the Arabs. This was to no avail, as the emperor now turned to acts of peace, proving to be wise and mild: to those who wanted him to draw up harsher laws to punish crimes against property, he replied, "We shall reduce expenditure, we shall diminish taxes, we shall only use honest functionaries, so that the people can have enough to eat and wear. This will lead to the end of theft and brigandage, more than any drastic punishment."

Thanks to the peaceful situation on the domestic and foreign fronts and to good government, China prospered and exported its products, rice, wheat, silk, spices, spending the proceeds to improve standards of living. The silk factories of the capital Chang'an employed 100,000 workers, and in winter most of the population wore furs; this affluence brought with it a love of luxury, beauty, poetry. The works of 2300 poets have been handed down, among which the writings of Wang Wei, Li Bai and Du Fu stand out. A well-turned verse or a good painting could earn its author an important post.

The Tang dynasty was temporarily eclipsed in 690, when an unprecedented event took place. The Empress Wu, instead of merely managing policy as ruler in the name of the underage emperor, seized power herself and set up her own dynasty, the Zhou. It died with her in 705, and the empire returned to the Tang. But this precedent would inspire several empresses in the centuries to come, and Empress Wu lives on in novels as the archetype of female debauchery, dedicated to pleasures of the flesh with monks and favorites.

In 712, Xuanzong was proclaimed emperor: his forty-year reign is considered to be the pinnacle of the Tang dynasty. An arts lover, he surrounded himself with poets and philosophers and wrote poetry himself. He abolished the death penalty and reformed prisons and courts; he enforced merciless taxation, but had moralistic aspirations, and forbade lady courtiers to wear jewellery and embroidered clothes. At the age of sixty, he fell in love with the twenty-six-year-old Yang Yuhuan (known as *Guifei*, "precious consort"), who was a concubine of his eighteenth son: this was the beginning of one of the most tragic and famous courtly tales. Taking advantage of the Son of Heaven's senile passion, the deadly Yang's relatives assumed the roles of masters; one of her brothers, who was corrupt and inept, governed with full powers, while Xuanzong spent day and night in Yang's arms. Yang Yuhuan had another suitor, An Lushan; he was a general of Tartar origins, and as governor of the northern provinces led the best imperial armies. In 755, driven by love, as literary tradition would have it, or by his hunger for power if historiographers are to be believed, he rebelled; with his 200,000 men he marched on Luoyang and then on Chang'an, which fell the following year. Once he had entered the capital, An Lushan declared himself emperor. Xuanzong fled after his soldiers had mutinied, killed Yang Guifei and her infamous brother before his very eyes, and then abandoned themselves to a general slaughter of the five families which made up the concubine's clan and which

had devoured the empire. The old, desperate Xuanzong abdicated, while An Lushan's troops, which mainly consisted of Tibetans, Turkic groups and Uygurs, sacked and destroyed Chang'an. It has been estimated that during the revolt and the civil war that followed, 36 million people lost their lives. In 757 a Tang army, also made up of barbarians, defeated An Lushan's troops and killed him. But only five years later, once the unrest had brought itself to an exhausted halt, could Xuanzong, now emperor again, return to the ruins of his capital, where he died a few months later.

The Tang dynasty never recovered from this shock, even though it remained in power for another century. In 874 a revolt of starving peasants spread throughout eastern China and shook the empire to its very foundations. They were led by Huang Chao, a scholar who had failed in his attempt to pass the state examinations and secure bureaucratic employment. Moving northward, he took Luoyang in 880 and Chang'an in the following year. Forced to flee, the emperor turned to the Turkic barbarians for help, and in 883 they won back the capital city for him. Huang Chao was killed, but the war started by Zhu Quanzhong, who placed a young boy on the throne, forced the boy to abdicate in Zhu Quanzhong's favor in 906. However, his dynasty, the Liang, did not last long and was limited to northern China, while the rest of the country was divided up among the potentates of the Five Dynasties and the Ten States.

After fifty years of chaos, a new unifier emerged, Zhao Kuangyin, who became Emperor Taizu. In less than two decades he managed to conquer most of the other kingdoms and founded the Song dynasty, making Kaifeng the capital city.

This was the beginning of what is generally referred to the as the Chinese renaissance, the first period of which was dominated by Wang Anshi, a reformer called to the government in 1067. Even his enemies, of whom there were many, recognized that he was an extraordinary man. He was so dedicated to the well-being of the people that he did not bother about his own appearance or clothes; he was an erudite man who, instead of immersing himself in his studies far from the troubles of the world, had gone into battle against the rich and powerful. The foundation of his doctrine was that the imperial government should be responsible for the well-being of all its subjects and should prevent one class from exploiting another, weaker one. He began by abolishing the obligatory forced labor that took peasants away from the fields precisely during the crucial sowing and harvesting periods; at the same time, to give the underprivileged masses employment, he launched huge public works for the canalization and control of the rivers to avert the frequent, devastating floods.

The state made loans to farmers at minimum interest rates, freeing them from the moneylenders who drove them into poverty; subsidies were given to the elderly and free seeds were given to those who could not afford to buy their own. The government set salaries and prices, and the state purchased all produce to sell it later at fair prices.

Reforms were made to the system of exams that scholars had to pass to become functionaries. History, geography and especially economics replaced rhetoric and stylistic virtuosity. Wang Anshi reduced the size of the army in order to economize, but decreed that each family that contained more than one adult male had to provide a soldier in the case of war. The state's horses and their fodder were entrusted to the peasants, who could use the horse to work their fields, but then had to return them to the armies when they were needed for military use.

As is often the case, these reforms, which seemed perfect on paper, met with many difficulties in their practical application. In addition to the rich, who were directly damaged in their desire for gain, Wang Anshi's measures also provoked opposition among those who benefited from them. The vast and deeply corrupt bureaucracy of functionaries lost the advantages that it had gained from the previous turmoil. Though freed from their forced labor, the peasants were unhappy; in exchange they had to pay modest taxes with which the state guaranteed services that they themselves had been required to provide before. Furthermore, the weight of tradition was so crushing that the conservatives had no problems in promoting their agenda of reversals; their rebellion forced Wang Anshi to resign in 1076.

Called back to power two years later, he lost his position for good in 1085 as a result of pressure from his adversaries, who also secured the abolition of his laws. However, some of his work remained; and the reformers, who were his followers, returned to power in 1093. In the meantime, though, Wang had died, and the new head of the reformist movement, Cai Jing, was not up to the same standard. Historians, who traditionally side with the conservatives, condemn him harshly as the person most responsible for the dynasty's downfall; they argue that he should have called the troops back from the northern frontiers to crush peasant revolts provoked by the unfavorable economic situation.

In the meantime, beyond the Great Wall, the power of the Jurchen nomads was growing; in Manchuria they founded the empire of Jin and once they had realized how weak China was, they moved across the border in 1126, conquered the capital Kaifeng and captured the emperor himself. The Song, having lost the whole of northern China, retreated beyond the Yangtze, where they managed to halt the invaders. A century later, the Jurchen invaders were struck by a storm that was to change the face of central-eastern Asia and of half of Europe: the Mongols, guided by Genghis Khan, overturned the Jin and for five years razed the northern regions to the ground. Ninety Chinese cities were so radically destroyed that "the cavaliers could cross them in the dark of night without fearing any obstacle." Death prevented the great slaughterer from finishing his conquest; it was his successors Ogodai, Mangu and Kublai who continued the devastating assaults.

When Kublai Khan's armies reached the walls of Canton, the last refuge of the last of the Song dynasty, the Chinese general Lu Xiufu tried to escape by sea with the boy-emperor; but when he saw that his ship was surrounded by Mongol vessels, he took the child in his arms and jumped into the sea. It is said that a hundred thousand Chinese followed his example, rather than give in to the invaders.

The erudite Wen Tianxian, brought before the Kublai after three years of imprisonment, was asked what he wanted in exchange for supporting the new regime. He answered, "I was minister under the Song, I cannot serve two masters. I ask only to die." While the executioner was sharpening his axe, he bowed down once more toward the south, as though his emperor still reigned in Nanjing.

38 THE POLOS WERE RECEIVED WITH THE HIGHEST
HONOURS AT THE COURT OF KUBLAI KHAN.
HAVING SET UP THE CAPITAL IN PEKING, THE
MONGOL DYNASTY, WHICH TOOK THE CHINESE
NAME OF YUAN, HAD A VAST COMPLEX OF IMPERIAL
PALACES BUILT IN THE CENTRE OF THE CITY.

39 HAVING BEEN STARTED BY GENGHIS KHAN, THE
CONQUEST OF CHINA WAS COMPLETED AFTER HIS
DEATH BY KUBLAI, THE "GREAT DOG" DESCRIBED BY
MARCO POLO, WHO WITH HIS BOOK "THE TRAVELS
OF MARCO POLO" INTRODUCED THE EUROPEANS TO
THE GLORIES OF THE MONGOL EMPIRE.

The Mongols, whose dynasty took the name Yuan, chose Peking as their capital, near to the steppes where they came from. Kublai turned that small provincial town into the largest and most ostentatious city in the world, the city which dazzled Marco Polo, who with his book *The Travels* introduced China to the Europeans for the first time. Once the Mongols had exhausted their desire for destruction during the terrible early stage of their conquest, they took on Chinese ways like all the previous invaders of China had done. Kublai kept the highest positions for his compatriots, but the inexperience of these warrior nomads meant that he had to rely on the Chinese bureaucracy to rule the vast empire. He attempted to expand his new empire even further, with expeditions to Vietnam, Korea, Cambodia, Burma and the islands of Japan. These were not always successful. In fact, his attempt to conquer Japan failed miserably: storms destroyed the Mongols' fleets.

Kublai (1215-1294) was the most extraordinary character in the Mongol dynasty. In the course of his thirty-four-year, and particularly after he had conquered the South, he tried to bring the conquerors and the conquered together in a new imperial structure. An intelligent admirer of Chinese culture, which he felt to be superior to his own, he surrounded himself with advisors of every race and religion: he appreciated Mongols and Chinese, Central Asian Muslims, and Europeans like Marco Polo for their abilities. The forceful Kublai had the Imperial Canal rebuilt; he extended and improved the road network and set up a postal service, which became the most efficient and speedy in the world of that era. He built public granaries for gathering the crop surpluses, which would then be distributed for free to the poor should there be famine. Peasants affected by drought, flooding or other natural disasters such as locust invasions were exempted from tax, while the elderly, orphans and the infirm were given state assistance. The subjects of the empire were divided into four classes. At the top, of course, were the conquerors, the Mongols, whose princes were given entire districts as their prerogative, and received all tax income from them. There were a few hundred thousand Mongols an overall Chinese population of sixty million. Then came the so-called "people of special grade," in other words the Mongols' allies and the functionaries that had come from all over Asia. They worked as administrators and dealt with finance and trade, organizing the caravans that traveled over the vast lands that enjoyed the Pax Mongolica. The third class was the *hanren*, a term that meant Chinese, but actually included all the subject peoples to the north of the Yangtze, from the Koreans to the Kitans. Finally, there were the *manzu*, meaning "barbarians of the south," those who lived in the ruined Song empire, who were in theory excluded from state employment; in practice, this rule was often broken by the well-intentioned Kublai. Below these four categories were the slaves, who had been reduced to a condition of servitude since the first stages of Mongol domination. Despite the Kublai's benevolent rule, the Mongols were nevertheless unable to endear themselves to their subjects. For the entire duration of the dynasty, they lived in China as though they were camping in a country that they did not understand and that they merely exploited, while the intrigues of their aristocracy tore the court to pieces. The last Yuan ruler, Togham Temur, who reigned from 1333 to 1368, had spent his childhood in a Buddhist convent in the far south of China; he had been sent there by his enemies in the hope that he would collapse in the tropical climate. He survived to take the throne thanks to another court faction; as he was influenced by the religious education that he had received, he was later subject to the influence of Tibetan lamas who introduced mystical-sexual orgies to the palace, which he and his entourage engaged in with abandon. Meanwhile, troubles broke out in the provinces. The peasant masses rebelled, having been made to provide forced labor to repair the embankments wrecked by the flooding of the Yellow River. The transport of cereals along the Imperial Canal was interrupted, and the capital was reduced to starvation. It was an outburst of social discontent against all rich people, whether they were Chinese or Mongols. But when Zhu Yuanzhang, a former monk of lowly origins, became leader of the rebellion, it became much more like a war of liberation against foreigners. After ten years of victories, Zhu declared himself emperor in Nanjing, founding the Ming Dynasty, and in 1368 he took Peking; Togham Temur had to flee back to the steppes, where he died two years later.

40 IN 1368, A REVOLT CRUSHED THE MONGOLS AND BROUGHT THE MING DYNASTY TO POWER, UNDER WHICH CHINA HAD A PERIOD OF MILITARY AND MARITIME EXPANSION: DELEGATIONS OF SUBJECT PEOPLES ARRIVED IN PEKING, SUCH AS THE GROUP SHOWN IN THIS PAINTING ATTRIBUTED TO SHANG XI (15TH CENTURY), BRINGING THEIR ANNUAL TRIBUTE TO THE EMPEROR.

The victor reorganized the empire on the model of the Song administration, but strengthening central power even further; Zhu's iron fist re-established peace all over China. The country had a new economic flowering, thanks also to the redistribution of the land that had been abandoned after the previous owners had fled or died. The clusters of Mongols who had remained scattered over the vast country were quickly assimilated through a law that imposed mixed marriages. Zhu died in 1398, after a thirty-year reign during which he had become increasingly morbidly suspicious, periodically indulging in purges of courtiers or functionaries. By the time of his death, China had once again become a large, strong, prosperous state. And under Zhu Di (Emperor Yongle), who came to the throne in 1402 after a brief war of succession between relatives, the country also became a maritime power. Indeed, between 1405 and 1433, impressive naval expeditions were organized, mainly run by the eunuch Zheng He, a Muslim from Yunnan. These expeditions took the Chinese fleets not only to the Indonesian archipelago and to India, but as far as the Persian gulf, in the Red Sea (where the pious Zheng He disembarked to make a pilgrimage to Mecca), and along the east coast of Africa. There, the eunuch admiral sought out the mythical unicorn; he did not find any, but brought an animal back to Nanjing that had never been seen before – the giraffe. This expansionist gesture, which could have had huge political and trading consequences, was limited to no more than an enlargement of geographical and zoological knowledge; the voyages were swiftly suspended with the death of Emperor Yongle and after Zheng He had returned from his last trip. The vast ocean junks rotted in the harbors, and from then on Chinese sailors limited themselves to coastal traffic. Japanese merchants were the first to take advantage of the situation, followed by the Portuguese, whose ships dropped anchor off Canton for the first time in 1517. Initially both were granted permission to trade, Initially they had permission to trade, but following friction and unrest they were driven away. From then on, for a good half century, the Japanese disturbed the Chinese coast with continuous acts of piracy, and also occupied some ports; meanwhile, in 1557 the Portuguese managed to occupy Macau. In 1592 and again in 1597, the Japanese also attempted to invade Korea, a vassal state of China, but the Chinese and Koreans pulled together and managed to crush them. In the north, the Ming had to confront the threat posed by the Mongols. After a period of civil wars, the Mongol tribes had united once more and were making incursions into the border provinces. The Chinese armies reacted with several retaliatory expeditions, but in 1449 Emperor Yingzong (Zhengtong), who had taken command of the troops, was defeated and made prisoner; he was only able to secure his freedom by paying a huge ransom. The conflict with the Mongols continued with a series of incidents until the end of the 16th century. However, in Manchuria at the end of that century, a Tungu people was strengthening its power. This people, the Manchu, would prove to be fatal to the Ming dynasty. To defend imperial territory, the Ming rebuilt most of the Great Wall and extended it; it took on the appearance that is admired today.

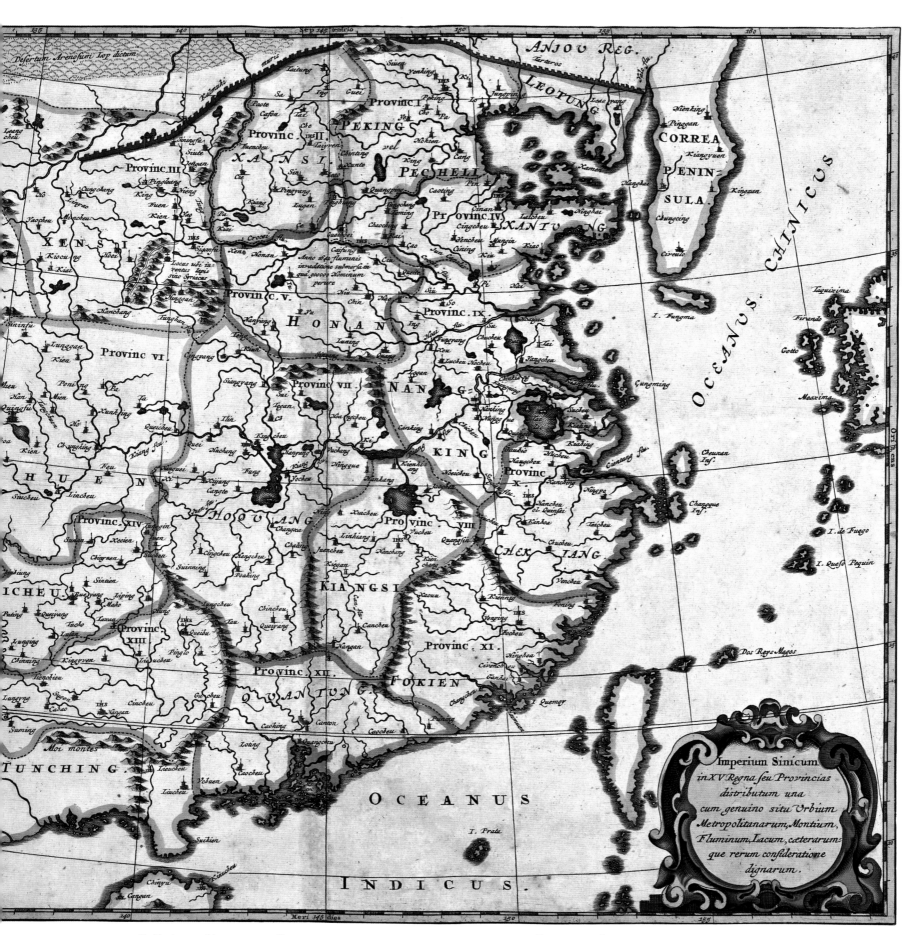

40-41 In the 16th century, Portuguese seafarers encountered the coasts of China, while Jesuit missionaries attempted to penetrate inland.

Thanks to information from them, in European atlases the Celestial Empire began to take on a dimension and shape that was fairly close to reality.

42 In 1644, taking advantage of civil strife, the Manchu took Peking and founded a dynasty there, called Qing, meaning "Pure". The second emperor, Kangxi, shown in this portrait, reigned for sixty years (1662-1722); this was perhaps the most prosperous and peaceful time in China's history.

43 Qianlong, the fourth Manchu emperor, shown here as a warrior, also had a very long and happy reign (1736-1795), bringing Chinese expansion to the peak of its power with the subjection of Xinjiang.

In the first decades of the 17th century, the central power in China found itself at the mercy of the intrigues of the eunuchs and the battle that they fought against the Confucian functionaries. In addition, an economic crisis provoked peasant uprisings, and concurrently the government was not able to end the nomads' challenges to the security of the borders. As a result, there was a revolt led by Li Zicheng: in 1644; having beaten the imperial armies, he entered Peking, where the last Ming emperor had hanged himself, after ordering his wife to kill herself. But on the northern frontier there was still a legitimist army whose commander called on the Manchu for help. They accepted; but once they had beaten the usurper and taken Peking, instead of restoring the fallen dynasty as they had agreed, they set up their own, which they called Qing, meaning "Pure." Three years later, the conquest of China was completed with the fall of Canton.

Despite the enforcement of some humiliating laws under which the Chinese suffered – such as the outlawing of mixed marriages and the requirement to wear their hair in a queue (pony tail) – they adapted to the new invasion, in part because the Manchu brought back order and well-being. Their first emperor, Shunzhi (1644-1661), young and sickly, wanted to learn the language of the conquered Chinese; in addition, he surrounded himself with the best minds of the Manchu aristocracy, governing with intelligence. His third-born son Kangxi was called upon to succeed him; he had contracted smallpox as a child and recovered from it, and therefore he seemed likely to live for a long time. Indeed, he reigned for sixty years, and gave China the most prosperous and peaceful period in her millenary history. At just fourteen years of age, Kangxi began ruling alone, releasing himself from all supervision. Energetic, active, thirsty for knowledge, he loved to live frugally. He traveled all over the empire, which now stretched from Tibet to Korea, from Turkestan to Annam, righting wrongs and taking an interest in the welfare of his people. He was a protector of the arts and literature,

and he spoke Mongolian, Tibetan, Manchu and Chinese. He also wished to learn Latin from the Jesuits who had established themselves at the court during the time of the Ming, in the hope of Christianizing China, and whom he admired for their scientific knowledge, In fact, he had been cured of malaria by their medicines. The reports that these missionaries sent to Europe stirred the admiration of the West for this empire ruled by a philosopher and administered by a bureaucracy whose members were selected on the basis of their literary merit. Throughout the whole of the 18th century, China was fashionable among cultivated Europeans; from that far-off land came excellent products such as silk, lacquerware, porcelain, and tea. Kangxi died in 1722; some maintained that he was poisoned by one of his fifteen sons, who was exasperated by his father's longevity, which prevented him from becoming emperor. This son was Yongzheng, who succeeded to the throne and ruled until 1735; although he was less friendly than his great father he was no less beneficial for the empire: he could not stand corruption, and imposed controls on all the functionaries, often using spies. He also reduced the feudal power of the Manchu princes, forcing them to live at court under surveillance. Yongzheng's fourth son Qianlong was also to have a very long reign, from 1736 to 1795. He considered himself the first servant of his subjects, and took on intense, untiring work every day. He also knew to surround himself with experts and skilled statesmen, at least in the first years of his reign. Unfortunately in his old age he let himself fall under the damaging influence of a general named Heshen, described by Chinese historians as a villain; when given the task of subduing a Muslim revolt in Gansu, he dragged out the operation in order to earn more money. However, it was under Qianlong that the Manchu dynasty reached its peak: with over 300 million inhabitants, the Chinese Empire at that time was the richest and best governed in the world. But soon later, the impact of European powers that were intent on imposing their "civilization" was to devastate it.

44 TOP In the Nineteenth century, European powers took advantage of their technological superiority to enforce their will upon the Chinese empire, which was reluctant to open up to foreign trade. Canton, where we see an English warehouse, was the only city in which foreign merchants could trade.

44 BOTTOM To force China to allow opium trading, in 1840 the French and the English organised an armed expedition that bombed several Chinese ports. In this painting by Edward Duncan (1803-1882), the English frigate Nemesis sinks several junks in the Bay of Anson (left).

45 While the empire wavered under attack from the west, the Taiping peasant revolt spread through the central and eastern provinces, and almost brought about the fall of the dynasty, which in this case had the support of the Europeans against the rebels (left). As the Chinese were unwilling to observe the treaty drawn up after the first Opium War, from 1856 to 1860 a second war was fought, which ended with the Franco-British troops marching on Peking, and the barbaric destruction of the Summer Palace (right).

At the end of the 18th century, Britain's East India Company enjoyed absolute domination among the European powers that traded with China, exporting tin, lead, wool and cotton fabrics, and importing tea in such great quantities that the balance of trade was largely in favor of the Celestial Empire. To remedy this unfavorable economic situation, the British began to sell opium produced in India on the Chinese market. Notwithstanding the severe imperial bans on using it as anything other than a medicine, use of the drug soon spread, encouraged by the corruption of the Chinese customs authorities, who made large profits from contraband. Imports rose from 200 baskets a year in 1729 to 40,000 in 1838. As early as 1825, the Chinese balance of trade was suffering, and the figures worsened every year. The imperial government decided to intervene drastically; they enforced compliance with the bans and appointed the mandarin Lin, the most ferocious opponent of opium trafficking, as commis-

sioner in Canton, which was the only port in which Europeans could trade. Commissioner Lin acted with untiring energy. He had all the secretly imported opium that had accumulated in the warehouses of Canton seized and burned, and in May 1839 he drove the British merchants out. The extremely powerful East India Company complained vociferously in the name of free trade, and the British government decided to retaliate with an armed expedition to force the Chinese to let themselves be drugged without protest or action. This was the first Opium War: the Royal Navy bombarded and occupied various Chinese ports from 1840 to 1842. In the end, China was forced to sign the Treaty of Nanjing, which stated that the Celestial

Empire had to cede the island of Hong Kong to Britain; it also paid a large indemnity and opened up four other ports to foreign trade, including Shanghai.

The second Opium War was fought between 1856 and 1860, to enforce compliance with the previous treaty and with the legalization of the opium trade. This time the British, allied with France, struck more harshly; they marched on Peking and with unjustifiable barbarity they destroyed the Summer Palace, one of the wonders of the world, after having looted it thoroughly. Meanwhile, a large popular uprising shook the central and southern provinces: a young fanatic who had mixed with Protestant missionaries and declared himself to be the younger brother of Jesus Christ intensified the dissatisfaction of the peasant masses. The rebels beat the imperial armies, took Nanjing, declaring it the capital of the new Taiping dynasty (meaning "Great Peace"), and threatened Peking. The last moments of the Manchu seemed to have arrived, but the European powers refused to ally with the revolutionaries, whose doctrine demonstrated dangerous traces of communism; instead, they took the side of the reigning dynasty, providing it with military assistance. Due in part to disputes that arose among their leaders, and their incapability to win over the northern populations, the Taiping were finally defeated and wiped out.

THE DOWAGER EMPRESS CIXI RULED CHINA IN THE SECOND HALF OF THE NINETEENTH CENTURY, WHEN THE COUNTRY WAS FORCED TO ENDURE THE INVASION AND INCREASINGLY OVERBEARING BEHAVIOUR OF THE EUROPEANS AND THE JAPANESE, WHO WERE FIGHTING FOR CONTROL OF THE CELESTIAL EMPIRE.

IN 1900 THE XENOPHOBIC REVOLT OF THE BOXERS SHOOK CHINA; THE QUARTER OF THE LEGATIONS IN PEKING, IN WHICH THE WESTERNERS TOOK REFUGE, WAS BESIEGED FOR 55 DAYS. IN THE PHOTO, FRENCH TROOPS DEFEND A BARRICADE IN TIANJIN, WHICH WAS ALSO BESIEGED BY THE REBELS.

The end of the Manchu dynasty was merely postponed, however. Unable to deal with the progressively more arrogant behavior of the "white devils" and incapable of modernizing the empire to enable it to defend itself, the regime suffered increasingly greater humiliations. Russia forced China to cede its territories north of the River Amur and east of the Ussuri; France imposed its own protectorate on the states of Indochina, which had been vassals of the empire; Japan took the island of Formosa and Korea, and Germany, France and Britain obtained other scraps of Chinese territory "in concession." Meanwhile Russia installed itself in Manchuria, where a few years later it would fight a bitter war with the Japanese for possession of that vast territory. The imperial government, led by the Dowager Empress Cixi, was paralysed by the struggle between reformers and traditionalists, while in the provinces the domineering behavior of the foreigners and the invasion of the missionaries (often only capable of offending the Chinese mentality with their superior attitudes) provoked a violent xenophobic reaction. The Fists of Righteous Harmony, a secret society known to westerners as the "Boxers," had become widespread in northern China. In 1900 it openly revolted against the "white devils" and the even more despised Japanese. The Boxers slaughtered merchants, missionaries and Chinese converts in various cities, and in Peking they besieged the area reserved for the Legations, where the foreigners barricaded themselves while they waited for help. Help arrived after 55 days in the form of an international expeditionary corps made up of British, French, Russian, German, American, Japanese and Italian troops; meanwhile, the imperial court, having oscillated between open support for the Boxers and an ambiguous policy of waiting, fled to faraway Shenxi. Once again, the victors' vendetta was merciless: the Forbidden City and Peking were sacked, and indiscriminate killings and rapes crowned the triumph of Western civilization.

47 LEFT The Boxers' revolt was mercilessly repressed in the bloodiest ways. This photograph shows the public beheading of a rebel captured in a village inland.

47 RIGHT Pu Yi, the last emperor of China, was deposed by the 1911 revolution but lived on for many years in the Forbidden City; he was then taken by the Japanese and installed on the throne of Manciukuo, Manchuria, as puppet ruler of the occupiers.

Severe reparations were imposed on China, which was now completely exhausted. At this point, aggressive Western politicians talking about dividing the empire among the European powers and Japan, as the Manchu dynasty had lost all credibility. The Chinese believed that the "mandate of Heaven" that had legitimized the dynasty in their eyes had been taken away, and that it should be replaced by a new regime. A revolutionary movement formed among the young people who had been sent abroad to England, Germany, America and Japan and who, upon their return to China, became increasingly irritated by the condition their country was in. The movement was led by a doctor, Sun Wen (Sun Yat-sen in his native Cantonese dialect), who in 1895 had already led an attempted uprising that had immediately been stifled. In 1911, the imperial government's request for a loan from the European powers led to intense opposition that became a mutiny in some quarters of the army, which had been influenced by anti-Manchu propaganda. The rebels occupied Nanjing and declared a republic, electing Sun Wen as provisional president. Lacking in any support, the imperial court surrendered. On the 12 February 1912 the last emperor, the boy Pu Yi, abdicated; he was allowed to remain in the Forbidden City in a sort of limbo. The revolutionaries proved to be less magnanimous in the provinces, where many Manchu were massacred. The brand-new republic immediately ran into difficulties. A general called Yuan Shikai was plotting to take power and found a new dynasty. Sun Wen was an honest, sincere idealist, but only an indifferent statesman. China disintegrated into a mosaic of provinces governed by the "war lords": soldiers of fortune who seized power by enlisting personal armies and imposing levies on the population. Desperate, the people turned to brigandage, while unscrupulous Europeans and Americans speculated by trafficking in arms and opium. In 1931 in Henan province alone, there were four hundred thousand bandits.

Military advisers were sent from Russia, where in the meantime the Bolshevik revolution of 1917 had triumphed. These advisers put together and trained a Nationalist army led by Jiang Jieshi (Chiang Kai-shek). From Canton the army marched on the northern regions and took Peking, but Jiang Jieshi turned against the Communists, crushing them at Shanghai, and set up a military dictatorship, supported by the western powers. Meanwhile, Japan decided to take advantage from the chaotic situation into which that China was heading: in 1931 the Japanese occupied Manchuria. They declared it to be independent, with the name Manchukuo, and placed Pu Yi, the last of Manchu dynasty, at the head of the state as a puppet-emperor. Then in 1937 the Japanese began to conquer China, taking Shanghai and moving back up the Yangtze valley as far as Nanjing; there, much of the civil population was killed indiscriminately while Jiang Jieshi's government withdrew to remote Chongqing. In 1940 the Japanese installed a puppet government headed by Wang Jingwei, but they never managed to take control of the vast Chinese territory, and limited their occupation to the eastern provinces.

Meanwhile the Communists, led by Mao Zedong, had brought their army from south to north on the epic Long March; they took command of the anti-Japanese resistance and won the support of the peasant masses. When Japan, having been beaten in the Second World War, had to leave China, Jian Jieshi was elected president of the republic at Nanjing, but the Communists formed their own government and occupied all the northern provinces. Their armies spread and took Shanghai and Nanjing, while the Nationalist army broke up, despite the fact that it had a plentiful supply of American arms. Jiang Jieshi and the last of his followers took refuge in Taiwan (Formosa), which remained separated from China from then on. On the 1 October 1949 in Beijing (formerly Peking), the People's Republic of China was declared, and Mao was elected its president.

Since then China, initially closely allied to the Soviet Union in the communist sphere but later its rival for hegemony over the communist movement, has returned to its role as a great international power; to do this it has undertaken the enormous task of reconstruction and economic development. Under Mao's leadership, the Chinese Communist Party unreservedly used propaganda and more or less forced mobilization, implementing agricultural collectivization and promoting industrial projects that required a numerous workforce and changed the face of entire regions, not always for the better. The energy plans increased oil and coal production, and hydroelectric and nuclear power plants were built. From 1957 to 1959 there was a voluntaristic effort to transform the Chinese economy from a rural to an industrial one, the so-called "Great Leap Forward." It failed, drastically reducing agricultural production and causing a famine that took 30 million lives. Similar disasters led to the Cultural Revolution, triggered by Mao in 1966, once again in the hope of solving new problems by suddenly erasing the millennia-old history of the nation. With the death of its historic leader in 1976, the Communist Party began liberal experiments that are still underway; these, however, did not prevent the bloody repression of a vast student protest in 1989, when hundreds of thousands of demonstrators gathered in Tian'anmen Square to demand reforms. China is now dealing with a difficult challenge: without renouncing communism, but rather maintaining the Party's control over society, the regime has promoted a renewal of society. This seems to be spurring the country's economic development on towards an unprecedented pace of growth, and there are many who predict that the ancient Middle Kingdom will play a hegemonic role in tomorrow's world. (G.G.)

THE HEART GIANT

THE HEART OF THE GIANT

As extensive as Europe, China has the third largest surface area in the world, ranking after Russia and Canada.

It has a solid continental form, with the exception of the Hainan Islands, which lie opposite Vietnam, and Taiwan, a breakwater between the East China Sea and the South China Sea; but in actual fact, along China's 3100 miles (5000 km) of rugged coastline there some 5000 smaller islands. This vast territory stretches from the deserts of Central Asia to the Yellow Sea, from the lightly inhabited Himalayan chain to the bustling plains of the east, from the torrid jungles on the border with Laos to the freezing steppes of Mongolia; it therefore includes a huge variety of landscapes. It has radically different ecosystems which move down from west to east in a sort of morphological scale made up of rugged mountain chains, from high altitude tablelands in the west, with the plateau of the central Yangtze valley, and the vast plains that jut into the Pacific Ocean to the east.

What could be called the water citadel of Asia is located in Chinese territory. Indeed, some of the continent's most important rivers originate on the Qinghai-Tibet plateau: the Mekong, which crosses Yunnan province and then enters Indochina and flows out into a delta in Vietnam; the Salween, which flows through Yunnan and Burma; the Indus, which runs through Kashmir to Pakistan and flows out into the Arabian Sea; the Brahmaputra, which runs down from Tibet to India and meets the Ganges in a vast delta on the Bay of Bengal; but above all, the Yangtze, also known as Chang Jiang (Long River) or the Blue River. This is China's longest watercourse: it is second only to the Nile in length, and is third in the world for its water flow rate. Its course — according to the most recent surveys — is 3900 miles (6300 km) long, about the same length as the Amazon River. The Yangtze rises in the Qinghai mountains on the Chinese-Tibetan border, and runs through tortuous canyons before forming the widest, most fertile valleys in the country; finally, it flows out into the East China Sea, just north of Shanghai. For an idea of the importance and size of the Yangtze, suffice to say that it reaches a fifth of Chinese land, runs through nine out of twenty-one provinces, provides 400 million people with water and is fed by no less than seven hundred tributaries.

China's second largest waterway is the Huanghe, or Yellow River. This rises in the west, in the Bayan Khara Ula massif; 3000 miles (4845 km) long, it slithers like a snake across northern China, first heading north toward the Gobi Desert, then south and then north again, finally coming out into the Gulf of Bohai, below Korea. Between about 7000 and 5000 B.C., the Neolithic cultures from which the Chinese civilization developed began in the Yellow River basin. Given the number of rivers China has, it is no surprise that the Chinese are the world's most skilled dam- and canal-builders: over half of the earth's 45,000 river weirs are found in China.

The first connections made between the ancient canals to create a navigable network to link north to south date back to the Sui dynasty (581-618 A.D.). The Grand Canal (or Imperial Canal) was completed in the 13th century to link the Yellow River with the Yangtze and other minor rivers; at 1112 miles (1794 km), it is the longest artificial waterway in the world. Through an intricate network of basins and canals, it links Beijing with Jiangsu and is an important communication channel, especially for transporting cargo. One of the canal's most attractive sections occurs where it flows through the southern provinces of Jiangsu and Zhejiang; charming cities such as Suzhou, Wuxi, Changzhou, Zhenjiang and Yangzhou have been built along its banks.

Considering the geophysical features of the region, we must not forget that two thirds of China's territory is made up of mountains, deserts, rocky tablelands, peat and steppes: these are harsh areas of land that are difficult or impossible to cultivate. This exacerbates the demographic pressure on the fertile third of the country, the irrigated plains of the center and south-east, while the immense, beautiful — yet unproductive — regions in the west and the far north remain mostly unpopulated. But the western provinces (Xinjiang, Qinghai, Tibet, Yunnan, Sichuan and Gansu) offer some of the most spectacular landscapes and the most incredible natural wonders. (M.M.)

56 This picture shows the top of Mount Siguniang, in Sichuan. Most of China's mountains are found in the western provinces, in other words Sichuan, Yunnan, Qinghai, Gansu and Tibet.

57 TOP LEFT Xinjiang has very varied landscapes, from lush forests to arid, semi-desertic areas like this, where erosion has caused unusual multicoloured rock formations.

THE WESTERN
REGIONS

In the northwest, in the Xinjiang ("New Frontier") Autonomous Region; on the border with Kazakhstan and immediately north of the Tianshan (Heavenly Mountains) range, is the Tarim basin; this vast mainly desert area is the largest inland basin on earth. In the basin's central section, the desolate moors and sand dunes of the Taklamakan extend limitlessly; at 128,000 sq. miles (320,000 sq. km), this is the largest desert in China and the second largest in the world. The eastern area differs; it is occupied by the endless saline region of Lake Lop Nor.

In the shelter of the Tianshan range lies the Turfan depression, an area of over 1600 sq. miles (4000 sq. km), most of which is 330 ft (100 m) below sea level. This area of China has the country's highest temperatures, often reaching over 45°C in summer. To the southeast of this desert area is the huge, inhospitable plateau divided between the province of Qinghai and the Tibet Autonomous Region. Situated at an average altitude of 14,850 ft (4500 m), it is mainly made up of stony deserts but is surrounded by splendid land-

scapes, with valleys overlooked by snowy peaks and monasteries in which a rigorous way of life is practiced.

The Himalayas are the most famous of the four main mountain chains that enclose Tibet; these also include the Kunlun, the Tanggula and the Kangdese-Nyainqentanglha mountains. These ranges are the highest part of a much more complex system of mountain chains produced during the Mesozoic era, which began some 250 million years ago with the closure of the Tetide, the ocean which divided Gondwana (the southern megacontinent) from Laurasia (the northern megacontinent). Evidence of the region's oceanic past remains in the form of numerous, large salt lakes without outlets: the Koko Nor (the Qinghai-hu), the largest, has a surface area of almost 2400 sq miles (6000 sq. km). With its mountain ridges rising to 19,800 ft (6000 m), with forty peaks of over 23,000 ft (7000 m) and with Mt. Everest at 29,028 ft (8846 m) in the Himalayas on the border of Nepal, Tibet is rightly considered to be "the roof of the world." Lhasa, the "city of gods," stands at an altitude of 11,880 ft (3600 m). For centuries it was a political,

57 TOP RIGHT The vast sandy expanses of the Taklamakan, the largest desert in the country, have earned it its reputation as "place of no return", especially due to the frequent sandstorms, or *buran*.

57 BOTTOM At the foot of Tianshan, ice covers the trees, turning them into spectral figures. The turquoise sky and bluish tone of the snow is a reminder that these remain the "Celestial Mountains".

cultural and religious capital, and is dominated by the Potala, the palace-monastery that rises on Marpori hill. The building has now been turned into a museum; its imposing white walls are bordered with blood red paint conceal the steps up which visitors ascend to visit the rooms where the Dalai Lama lived; they can also admire a splendid collection of sculptures, frescoes and *tangka*s, the typical Tibetan paintings on fabric. Each day the old city is crowded with pilgrims. Holding their prayer wheels, they walk clockwise around the Barkhor, the ring surrounding the Jokhang, the golden-roofed temple; they bow down in front of the main door of the temple, which is the most venerated Buddhist sanctuary in Tibet. The surrounding streets are the busy scene of a colorful market,

one of the most interesting in the region. In the Lhasa valley are the Drepung, Sera and Ganden monasteries. Drepung (5 miles (8 km) west of Lhasa, is surrounded by fertile land that once produced food for the monks. With its seven thousand monks, Drepung was the base of early Dalai Lamas before the Potala was built.

One of the most famous Lamaist temples is the Kumbum in Gyantse; it is built like a mandala on a cross-shaped plan that takes magical elements into account. Inside, visitors can admire a statue of the Buddha, covered in gold.

Quinghai province is a Tibetan natural heritage area; its name means "green sea" and derives from the name of Qinghaihu, the largest expanse of salt water in the country. It is in the northeast of the province, and is one of the region's most incredible natural spectacles. Its green-blue water, rippled by the breeze, reflects white clouds puffed by the wind, which seem to float in a clear sky, often darkened by flocks of birds.

Qinghai province contains one of the most important lamaseries, Ta'er; this monastery belongs to the reformed Buddhist sect of the Gelugpa ("the followers of virtue," also known as the "Yellow Hats"), which is the most recently formed but perhaps most representative order of Tibetan Buddhism. The reform in question was made in the 13th century by the master Tsongkhapa (1357-1419) and Ta'er was built at his birthplace, 16 miles (26 km) south of the provincial capital Xining. Qinghai is very large but only barely populated. It is still fairly backward in economic terms, but it has splendid flora and fauna. In summer, when the shepherds set up their tents in the huge emerald-green fields, with mountainous chains on the horizon, the area swarms with horses, sheep and cows out to pasture. Recently, however, many areas are threatened by desertification, which seems to be unstoppable. Huge parts of the province that used to be literally covered by a sea of grass rippling in the wind, are now struck by frequent periods of drought; during these periods, part of the livestock is lost due to the gradual disappearance of the grassy mantle and the resulting lack of forage. Clearly, this phenomenon also hits areas used for agriculture, and results in serious damage to the economy of these regions.

In addition to natural beauty, the province's strong point has always been its abundance of water resources. As was noted earlier, some of Asia's most important rivers originate from the Qinghai-Tibet plateau. Unfortunately, the widespread deterioration caused by desertification threatens Lake Qinghai itself, as well as the infrastructures for conserving and distributing water. Many of the lake's tributaries are often dry, so that the water level is falling each year with a constant rhythm.

Northeast of Qinghai, Gansu province and the Ningxia Hui Autonomous Region offer breathtaking scenery. This region was once traversed by the first stages of the Silk Route, the caravan paths that linked Asia and Europe for several centuries and promoted the flowering of trade between the Near East and China, especially during the Tang dynasty (618-907). Leaving from the capital Chang'an, now called Xi'an, the caravan trail headed westward across Gansu province; dividing into two branches at Dunhuang, it passed north and south around the outskirts of the Taklamakan Desert and then the trails joined up again at Kashgar. Not only did merchants and adventurers pass along these routes, but also monks from India who brought texts and images of Buddhist art to China, opening up the Far East to the message of the Enlightened One. With the spread of this new religion, various centers for Buddhist monks sprang up near the cities on the Silk Route. One of the largest is the rocky complex of Mogao, near Dunhuang, where hundreds of caves were dug out from the 4th century A.D. onward. Many of them were later destroyed by natural causes or by man, but 492 of them are still intact, with their priceless content of architecture, sculpture and painting.

Farther south, at the eastern border with Tibet, is Sichuan, a populous region that forms a sort of geographical and cultural belt between the west and east of the country. The province has some of the most spectacular landscapes in China, such as the national parks of Jiuzhaigou and Huanglong, which have been on the UNESCO World Heritage list since 1992. In the north of Sichuan, on the border with Gansu, Jiuzhaigou Park has one of the most extraordinary lake complexes in the world. In a vigorous backdrop of waterfalls, pine forests and snowy peaks that recall the United States' Rocky Mountains are over one hundred lakes, with transparent yet supernaturally blue water that changes shade in the course of the day. This spectacular phenomenon is caused by the presence of calcium carbonate. This is the same element that gives a turquoise color to the tens of wells that — at an altitude of 12,210 ft (3700 m) in nearby Huanglong National Park — lie among the hot sul-

fur springs. They can be reached by walking for two hours among azalea woods in the majestic scenery of the Min range. This mountainous chain gives its name to the river which, cutting through deep canyons, crosses many of the northern parts of Sichuan; these areas are partly inhabited by peasants and yak herders who belong to Tibetan minorities of the Qiang ethnic group.

But to return to Jiuzhaigou: in its 288 sq. miles (720 sq. km) of wild nature, a pathway unravels among sheets of water with romantic names and a magical appearance. There is the Lake of the Sleeping Dragon, whose imaginary shape can be made out among the fingers of land covered in vegetation, which jut into the cobalt-blue water; the Five Flowers Lake, surrounded by azalea forests with blooms of every color; the Five Colors Lake, which opens up at the foot of a steep path, from which its blue water appears like a mirage; and, hemmed in by snowy mountains, the Long Lake, on which romantic boat trips are available to visitors. Among the many waterfalls, the most spectacular are those at Nuorilang, the Pearl and the Panda; the latter is dedicated to the animal for which Sichuan is famous the world over. Indeed, this province is home to 80 percent of the thousand pandas that have survived in China. The visitor is unlikely to spot any in Jiuzhaigou. However, they can be seen up close in Chengdu, the provincial capital; a twenty-minute drive from the capital is the Chengdu Giant Panda Research Base, the laboratory reserve, where since 1987 a team of zoologists has been working on research and experiments to prevent the species from becoming extinct. Another feather in the cap of Sichuan province is the Dujiangyan irrigation system, one of the masterpieces of Chinese hydraulics technology and still working today. This network of canals, which date back to the 3rd century B.C., controls and distributes water from the Min river to irrigate the fertile plain of Chengdu.

At the end of the Tang dynasty (9th century A.D.) the ancient sculptures of the Dazu archeological complex were built. This complex northwest of Chongqing has over 40 different sites in which more than 50,000 sacred images were carved out of the rock. The sculptures are inspired by Taoist, Confucian and Buddhist iconography, and date from the Tang, Song (960-1279), Ming (1368-1644) and Qing (1644-1912) periods. The impressive figures at Dazu, such as the 102-ft-long (31 m) sleeping Buddha on Mt. Baoding, are an eloquent reminder of the religious syncretism that marks this country.

In the south west of Sichuan, at Leshan, is the most colossal Buddhist monument in the world. This is the Great Buddha, which stands out imposingly from the rock face on which it was carved, at the confluence of the Min, Dadu and Qingyi rivers. Work began on it in 713 A.D. during the Tang dynasty, and employed tens of thousands of workers for ninety years. The statue is huge: at 234.5 ft (71 m) high it is 60 ft (18 m) higher than the large sculpture of Bamiyan in Afghanistan (which the Taliban disfigured and shelled), and it is 92.5 ft (28 m) wide at the shoul-

fall, the luckiest among them can witness an extraordinary sight, a sort of mirage like a rainbow, locally called the "Buddha's aura" (*Foguang*); it is probably due to light being refracted through the clouds. In the past, more than one pilgrim fell victim to this romantic sight, and they say that some even threw themselves off the mountain, almost in response to some mysterious calling.

South of Sichuan, Yunnan province sits between Burma, Laos, Vietnam, Guangxi Autonomous Region and Guizhou province. Yunnan offers a surprising variety of scenery and ecosystems. They range from the humid tropical forests at Xishuangbanna on the border with Laos to the temperate plateau in the north, where Kunming, the provincial capital, is located. Before arriving in the city the visitor encounters the Shilin, or the Stone Forest. This is a kind of labyrinth of pinnacles made up of thousands of column-

like calcareous rock formations up to 100 ft (30 m) tall; eroded by the wind and rain, they create a bizarre, almost unreal sight. The discovery of marine fossils in the area shows that Yunnan, which is adjacent to Tibet, also used to be submerged in the Tetide ocean. North of Kunming the land rises up to 6600 ft (2000 m) to the Dali plateau, much of which is

ders. The ear lobes measure 23 ft (7 m) the big toes over 26 ft (8 m) and the fingernails 5 ft (1.5 m). The imposing Buddha faces Mt. Emei, in the county of the same name. This is one of the Buddhists' sacred mountains which, at 10,227 ft (3099 m) in height, overlooks the left bank of the Dadu river. There are about seventy sacred buildings in the area, which make it one of the most important religious complexes in the country. In China there are over two hundred mountains that are sacred to Buddhists, but four are pre-eminent, and each of them is associated as a place of meditation with one of the four most venerated bodhisattvas. The Emeishan is dedicated to the cult of Samantabhadra (literally: "he who has universal goodness"), called Puxian in Chinese. Once pilgrims reach the top, they salute the sunrise. At sundown, after a storm or snow-

covered by the peaceful Lake Erhai and it is also surrounded by nineteen peaks of marble, silica, limestone, gneiss and granite that soar to over 13,200 ft (4000 m). Northwest of Dali, which is situated in the center of the province and home to the Bai ethnic group, stand the three famous pagodas of the Chongsheng temple. The oldest, the Qianxun, was built in the 9th century in the Tang dynasty style, and is made up of sixteen levels rising to about 230 ft (70 m). Later, two smaller pagodas were built; they are only 139 ft (42 m) high. For a view over the landscape surrounding the regional capital Dali, it is possible to take a chair-lift up to the Buddhist temple of Zhonghe. From here, the so-called "Path of Clouds" can be followed on horseback; this is a mule-track paved with slabs of granite which, 8580 ft (2600 m) up, runs alongside the plateau for 11 miles (18 km) , with some breathtaking views.

Beyond the Dali area, is the Lijiang valley, in the northwest of the province. This region is a plateau at a height of 8580 ft (2600 m) high, surrounded by the mountain chain named Yulong Xueshan ("Snowy Mountains of the Jade Dragon"), which is dominated by a majestic 18,466 ft (5596 m) peak. The Mountains of the Jade Dragon boast the greatest botanical variety in the whole of Yunnan, which is known in the rest of China as the "Kingdom of Plants." In fact, this southern province is home to 6000 botanical species (about half of all so far catalogued in China as a whole), and its woodland paradise bursts with color in the springtime, with 60 varieties of azaleas, 100 types of orchid, 184 varieties of rhododendrons, and tulips of every imaginable hue. At the Lamaist Buddhist monastery of Yufeng, at the foot of the Jade Dragon, the legendary "Camellia of ten thousand blooms" can be admired. This is a knotty tree that was planted in 1465, during the Ming dynasty. For over one hundred days a year, it blossoms with eighteen-petaled blooms: it is a natural miracle that has become a place of pilgrimage. Lijiang is also a fascinating place to visit; it is a village of ancient wooden houses built among a series of canals that are crossed by stone bridges and walkways that lead to workshops and houses. It is an intriguing mix of corners of old China and slivers of daily life, and is now protected by UNESCO.

In the northwest of the Yunnan province, north of the Lijiang valley, beyond the rock-faced Tiger Gorge hollowed out by the Yangtze (and overlooked by a sculpture of the big cat), the visitor reaches the remote Zhongdian plateau. At 10,566 ft (3200 m) in altitude, it is the heart of the autonomous Tibetan prefecture of Deqen (or Diqing). Several sources have identified the Zhongdian area with the legendary Shangri-La, the place of eternal youth that James Hilton described in his novel *Lost Horizon* (1933), which Frank Capra made into a film of the same name in 1937. On this wide plateau, on which barley is grown with the help of yaks, human beings survive, partly thanks to the numerous hot water springs around which many villages have been built. This is where Songzanlin was founded in the 17th century – one of the most important Tibetan Buddhist monasteries, which now houses 1200 monks. From Zhongdian, a tortuous dirt track leads along the courses of the rivers Yangtze and Mekong, among villages built on the Himalayan slopes of the Deqen valley. Having made it through passes higher than 13,860 ft (4200 m), among pine and beech forests, speckled azaleas and clumps of red, pink, yellow and white rhododendrons, the visitor reaches the city of Deqen, which stands at 11,880 ft (3600 m), opposite the Kawa Gebo: this mountain, which rises to 22,240 ft (6740 m) in the center of the range of thirteen peaks that divides Yunnan from Tibet, is a cult place for Buddhists. Every morning from five o'clock on, pilgrims arrive. There on the mountain, among stupas, colored flags and rites of devotion, they watch spectacle of dawn lighting up the glaciers.

Another extraordinary natural sight is created by the so-called "three parallel rivers." Like many other rivers, the Jinsha, Lancang and Nujiang rise from the Qinghai-Tibet tableland and then run between the Yunnan mountains, one beside the other, never meeting.

This protected area is a true nature sanctuary and contains rare species of flora and fauna. Moving eastward from the marvelous landscapes of the west, the visitor comes to regions that are full of contradictions, where worlds that have remained unchanged since time immemorial live alongside futuristic cities and avant-garde industrial centers. (M.M.)

62-63 THE PHOTOGRAPH SHOWS EVEREST, THE HIGHEST MOUNTAIN IN THE WORLD, AT 8846 METRES. IT MARKS THE BOUNDARY BETWEEN THE CHINESE AUTONOMOUS REGION OF TIBET AND THE KINGDOM OF NEPAL.

64-65 Three yaks are carrying a load of goods to the Rongbur glacier, at the foot of Mount Everest. These bovines (which are native to the Himalayas) make daily life possible on the "Roof of the World".

66-67 This mountaineer's tent is at the foot of Mount Everest. The first person to conquer this mountain was the New Zealander Edmund Hillary, on 29th May 1953, together with the Nepalese sherpa Norgay Tenzing.

68-69 The peak of Mount Kawa Gebo, which is 6740 metres high, is found in the upper Deqen valley, on the border between Yunnan province and the autonomous region of Tibet. The Tibetan people that live in the area consider this mountain to be a divine manifestation.

70-71 The mountainous chain of Kunlun, in Xinjiang, stretches for 2500 kilometres from east to west, between Pamir and Sichuan. According to Taoist tradition, these peaks concealed the Western Paradise, a sort of Chinese Olympus reigned over by Xiwangmu, the Queen Mother of the West.

72-73 THIS TIBETAN WOMAN IS CROSSING A RIVER WITH A YAK. THE HIMALAYAN PEOPLES USE THESE ANIMALS TO TRANSPORT GOODS OR CULTIVATE BARLEY FIELDS.

74-75 THE MONASTERY OF DREPUNG, SITUATED 8 KILOMETRES WEST OF LHASA, MEANS "MOUND OF RICE", BECAUSE IT IS IN THE MIDDLE OF FERTILE LAND THAT PROVIDES THE MONKS WITH THEIR FOOD.

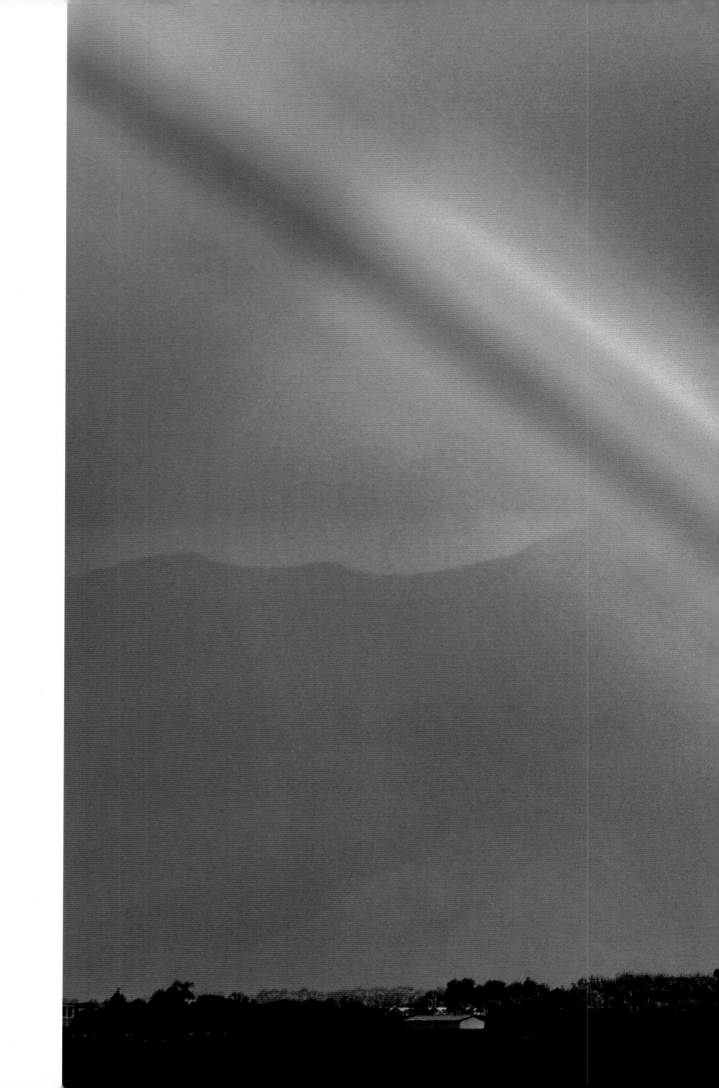

76-77 A BRIGHT RAINBOW ARCS INTO
THE SKY FROM MOUNT MARPORI;
THIS IS WHERE THE IMPOSING MASS OF
POTALA STANDS, LOOKING MORE LIKE A
FORTRESS THAN A PLACE OF WORSHIP.
ONCE THE RESIDENCE OF THE DALAI
LAMA, THE PALACE REMAINS THE MAIN
SYMBOL OF LHASA AND OF TIBET.

78-79 THE NORTH-WESTERN AUTONOMOUS REGION OF XINJIANG, WHICH MEANS "NEW FRONTIER", CONSISTS MAINLY OF DESERTS AND ARID MOUNTAINS, BUT THESE MAKE FOR SOME SPECTACULAR LANDSCAPES, ESPECIALLY AT DAWN AND AT DUSK.

80-81 REDUCED TO RUINS, THE CITY OF GAOCHANG, IN XINJIANG, WAS THE CAPITAL OF THE UYGURS. THE NOMADIC PEOPLE, OF TURKISH ORIGIN, FOUNDED THE CITY IN THE 9TH CENTURY WHEN IT MIGRATED TO THE REGION OF KAZAKHSTAN.

82-83 A PROCESSION OF CAMELS CROSSES THE DESERT NEAR DUNHUNAG; THIS IS THE OASIS OF THE NORTH-WESTERN PROVINCE OF GANSU, AND FOR CENTURIES IT WAS AN IMPORTANT CENTRE FOR CARAVANS ON THE SILK ROUTE.

84-85 In Yunnan there is
the Stone Forest (Shilin), a
labyrinth of pinnacles made
up of thousands of column-
like calcareous rock
formations up to 30 metres
tall; having been eroded by
the wind and rain, they
create a bizarre, almost
unreal sight.

86-87 These two women sit beside the turbulent waters of the Tiger Gorge, an impervious canyon hollowed out by the Yangtze river north of Lijiang, in northern Yunnan.

88-89 The Puzhehei plain, which lies 280 kilometres south-east of Kunming, recalls the Guilin area in Guangxi, with its rocky mounds covered in lush vegetation, its clear lakes and azure rivers.

90-91 This picture shows the extraordinary landscape of arid mountains alternated with lush green paddy fields in Luoping, in the south-western province of Yunnan, which is one of the most spectacular provinces in China.

92-93 The earth in the Dongchuan area in Yunnan province is rich in laterite. The green of the crops creates a strong colour contrast with this reddish, clayey land.

94 AND 95 THE WARM LIGHT OF SUNSET ON THE RICE TERRACES, THE FOG AT THE BOTTOM OF THE VALLEY
AND THE MOUNTAINS ON THE HORIZON TURN THESE LANDSCAPES IN YUNNAN INTO MASTERPIECES OF NATURE.

96 IN THE STRETCH BETWEEN GUILIN AND YANGSHUO IN GUANGXI PROVINCE, THE RIVER LI FLOWS BETWEEN KARSTIC FORMATIONS IN STRANGE SHAPES.

97 LEFT ROCKY PEAKS PIERCE THROUGH THE FOG IN THE COUNTY OF ZIYUAN IN GUANGXI PROVINCE, ONE OF THE MOST SPECTACULAR REGIONS OF CHINA.

97 RIGHT THE QUTANG GORGE IS THE FIRST OF THREE GORGES THAT ARE ENCOUNTERED WHEN MOVING DOWN THE YANGTZE FROM CHONGQING TOWARDS WUHAN.

SERPENTS
OF WATER AND ROCK

East of Yunnan province, in the Guangxi Autonomous Region, is the distinctive area of Guilin. Here, an endless sequence of mounds of calcareous formations, modeled into bizarre forms by wind and rain and covered in subtropical vegetation, has created one of the most majestic natural wonders in China. This strip of unusual hills, which is approximately 9.5 miles (15 km) wide, stretches from north to south for just over 50 miles (80 km) along the River Li, from the city of Guilin to the city of Yangshuo. For over a thousand years, a plethora of Chinese artists has depicted, evoked and sung of the Guilin area as one of the most beautiful places in the world. The southern part of the course of the Lijiang, toward Yangshuo, is startlingly beautiful, with the pointed silhouettes of the mountains contrasting with bamboo-covered riverbanks. There are villages of wooden houses, and children swimming to meet the passenger boats, as well as water buffalo and fishermen's boats. At nightfall, the men light the boat lanterns and go fishing in the traditional way, with cormorants. In this region human interactions with nature are among the most harmonious to be found in all China. The terracing of the hills for rice cultivation creates a charming effect.

North of Guangxi, Guizhou province, with its capital Guiyang, is a little off the beaten track for visitors. However, Guizhou holds unexpected surprises; a journey through this area is a memorable experience. The humid subtropical climate with its frequent rainfall encourages lush vegetation to develop, creating an extraordinary atmosphere. The area is all the more interesting for its pleasant succession of caves, forests, mountains and rivers, which together create a remarkable effect. This extraordinary karstic environment has the most impressive waterfall in China, the Huang-guoshu, which ranks among the most famous in the world.

East of Guizhou, Hunan has no less to offer in terms of natural beauty. Surrounded on three sides by mountains, it is delimited to the north by the Yangtze and Lake Dongting. Hunan, which is also renowned as the birthplace of Mao Zedong and other important revolutionaries, offers scenery that seems the ideal embodiment of the relationship between mountains and water that is the foundation of Chinese landscape painting. Hubei province, like Hunan, is cut through by the Yangtze. Here, in the middle of its course, the river has its most enchanting section: between Chongqing and Wuhan, the capital of Hubei, are the Three Gorges, a succession of dropping cliffs, rapids, bizarre rock formations and magical scenery. This route is covered every day, between March and November, by tens of cruise ships which leave from Chongqing harbor to reach first the Qutang gorge, 5 miles (8 km long), enclosed between jagged mountains that rise as high as 4124 ft (1250 m). The "serpent of water and rocks" then flows out into the Daxi valley, where oranges are grown. The next gorge, Wu, is 27 miles (44 km) long and is associated with the legend of a witch who is famous for having cured an ancient emperor with a potion of herbs. In fact, many of the plants that grow on the mountains are still used today in Chinese medicine. The third gorge, Xiling, is around 43 miles (70 km) long and has unusual rock formations, sudden shallows and turbulent currents. The greatest dam in history is being built on these banks, although the Herculean task has met with strong opposition from environmentalists. Water dominates yet another inland province, Anhui, east of Hubei, an agricultural region which has a very varied landscape. It is crossed by the river Huai in the north, and by the Yangtze in the south, two rivers that have often caused disastrous flooding. There are also a great number of lakes, of which Chaohu is the largest.

In the south if this province stands another of the sacred Buddhist mountains, Mt. Jiuhua, with its slopes dotted with ancient temples. This is the realm of Ksitigarbha ("he who has the earth as matrix"), known as Dizang in China; he is the bodhisattva of the Great Vow, a symbol of altruism. This is another area that emanates spirituality. Here again, water is the dominating element, with countless brooks, waterfalls and lakes.

In the southeast part of Anhui is the Huangshan ("Yellow Mountain"). It has been celebrated by poets and artists for its beauty; for its peaks with their romantic names, soaring above ancient pine trees and immersed in a sea of clouds and mist; and for its infinite variety of plants, its varied wildlife and its hot water springs with curative properties.

The southeastern provinces, along the middle and lower stretch of the Yangtze, are among the most developed in the country. Those that sit on the South and East China seas, especially, have always been the advantaged access point to China. From south to north, there is wealthy Guangdong, populous Fujian, Zhejiang with its countless islands and finally Jiangsu, "the Land of Water." The municipality of Shanghai is wedged between the latter two provinces. A journey through these lands reveals the most obvious signs of modernity and the race toward wealth, but it is also a magical trip across some of the symbolic places of Chinese spirituality: sacred mountains, lakes, rivers, enchanted villages.... Here, swarming human activity often gives way to spaces full of peace and spirituality. Some peaceful oases can also be found in nearby Guangdong, a province that is dedicated to productivity. For example, Zhaoqing, west of the capital city Guangzhou (Canton), is a charming town set among paddy fields; it is famous for Qixingyan, the "Rocks of Seven Stars" – seven crags that rise out of a lake, among caves, bridges and waterways. Or, for bird lovers, there is the Xinhui Bird Paradise, in the delta of the Pearl River, where lush tropical vegetation provides the setting for countless examples of a wide variety of species, especially herons.

Moving back up the coast to the northeast, we come to the inhabited Fujian province, with its capital Fuzhou. Many of the Chinese who emigrated abroad, came from this province. Fujian's vocation as a bridge toward the outside world has very ancient origins. For at least a thousand years, this area has been the southern portal of China for those arriving by sea. Together with the other coastal provinces of Guangdong and Zhejiang, it was also where the great Chinese navigators departed from to explore far-flung lands. Even before this, in Marco Polo's times, the city was one of the largest and busiest ports in the world, and rivaled Alexandria for its splendor. The Europeans called it Zaiton, from the Arabic. Diplomats, missionaries and merchants flocked here from all over, bringing with them their own customs and the most disparate creeds.

The Wuyi Mountains Natue Reserve, in the north of the province, has one of the most extraordinary subtropical forests on the planet. It is the ideal environment for rare species and subspecies of plants and animals. Some of the buildings on these mountains are particularly significant as they are associated with the origins of neo-Confucianism; this doctrine originated in China in the 11th century and was influential in eastern and southeastern Asia. In addition to the beauty of the scenery, these mountains are renowned for the excellent black tea that is produced there. The porcelain to which the country has even given its name ("china"), is associated with these places. Here in Fujian, in Dehua county, the *blanc de Chine* was made, white monochrome ceramics that became famous in Europe from the 17th century onward. Nearby Jiangxi province, inland, shares the same vocation; just a few hours journey from the capital Nanchang in the northeast, is Jingdezhen, still considered to be the "porcelain capital." Here, rich kaolin sediments encouraged the development of this industry as far back as a thousand years ago or more. Since then, the most Chinese ceramics have been produced here – among the best known is the "blue and white" – some of which were created for the imperial court. The local ceramics museum has some interesting exhibits from various eras, and illustrates every stage in the procedure for making porcelain. However, the most interesting thing is to observe the artisans at work. Although nowadays electric or gas kilns and modern lathes are widespread, it is still possible to find wood-burning kilns and potters who shape their pieces with traditional lathes or decorate them using ancient techniques. The kaolin quarries and the remains of the "dragon ovens" on the riverbanks can still be seen from the village of Yaoli, about 30 miles (50 km) from the city.

In this region, agriculture – particularly rice, with two harvests each year – thrives thanks to the fertile terrain and hot climate. The province has mainly hilly ground and is marked by some high peaks. In the north, the Lushan National Park surrounds Mt. Lu. Spectacular views can be seen from the mountaintop: the green ribbon of the Yangtze seems to

99 LEFT A FLEET OF TRADITIONAL BOATS WITH THEIR SAILS UNFURLED, ON THE YANGTZE AT NANJING, THE CAPITAL CITY OF JIANGSU PROVINCE.

99 RIGHT SHAOXING IS AN ANCIENT CITY IN ZHEJIANG, WHICH IS RENOWNED AS THE BIRTHPLACE OF LU XUN (1881–1936), ONE OF THE GREAT LITERARY FIGURES OF THE TWENTIETH CENTURY; HERE, THE ARCHITECTURAL STYLE IS TYPICAL OF THE CITIES OF JIANGNAN, A TERM USED TO INDICATE THE REGIONS "SOUTH OF THE RIVER" — THE RIVER BEING THE YANGTZE.

unravel across the plain toward the east, where Lake Boyang shines.

Boyanghu, nearby, is the largest freshwater lake in the country. Its mild climate means that each autumn thousands and thousands of migratory birds flock here from far-off Siberia, Mongolia, from the northern regions of China, from Japan and Korea, and then fly off in the spring; in both periods of the year, an impressive sight is guaranteed.

Returning to the coast, and then moving up toward the Yangtze and Shanghai delta, the visitor crosses Zhejiang. Hills and mountains cover around 70 percent of this province. There are also many bays and harbors, such as Wenzhou and Ningbo, that are important for international maritime trade. But it is the islands that that make this region so distinctive, as Zhejiang is the province with the most of them, along its jagged coastline stretching for more than 1240 miles (2000 km) on a sea filled with fish. On a small island in the Zhoushan archipelago, in the East China Sea, stands one of the four sacred mountains of Chinese Buddhism, the Putuo. Among the most interesting elements here, in addition to various panoramic spots and a colossal statue of the bodhisattva, are the three temples of Puji, Fayu and Huiji; these magnificent structures

are typical examples of the architectural style of southern China. However, what really makes this place so attractive is undoubtedly the magical union of the mountain and the waves, where water and sky meet.

Between the provincial capital Hangzhou and the coast is Shaoxing; it is a city of ancient renown. Shaoxing is crossed by a tightly-knit network of rivers, lakes and very busy canals on which water taxis run, covered with dark canvas: these are the *wupeng*, agile wooden boats that, for over a thousand years, have been plowing through the water of this ancient center, with its narrow cobbled streets. The capable boatmen who drive these unusual taxis use hands and feet to move along the waterways, holding on to banks and bridges. As it is a city on the water, Shaoxing has thousands of stone bridges, with different shapes and features; the bridges connect the streets, and cross over canals lined with ancient buildings with pale walls and dark tiled roofs. Picturesque, magical scenes are to be found all over Zhejiang province, thanks to the richness of its vegetation and the large number of forests, rivers and especially lakes. Like that of the capital Hangzhou, for example; or farther west, Qiandaohu, the "lake of a thousand islands": a gigantic mirror of water that is so clear it could almost be drinkable, scattered with little islands of different sizes, and surrounded by verdant hills. Innumerable tiny islands also dot the surface of Taihu, the third largest freshwater lake in China, between Zhejiang and Jiangsu. On the north bank of the lake is the city of Wuxi — "the pearl of Taihu" — which accommodates crowds of holidaymakers. Now we are in Jiangsu, a rich province on the Yellow Sea. The landscape is dominated by water: here too, there are a great number of lakes, rivers and artificial canals, such as the Grand Canal that crosses the region from north to south. The floating cities of the Jiangnan area, between Jiangsu and Zhejiang, with their rivers and canals, their bridges and boats, their wood and stone houses, their pavilions and secluded gardens, embody the ideal image of unchanging China. In these small cities, the culture of life on water still survives, with its traditions, simple and slow; and life continues to pulse along the banks of the canals, where women stoop to wash laundry or vegetables, or concentrate on buying goods from traveling salesman, looking over the canals from their windows. It is like plunging into a scroll painted with scenes of now bygone life, merging with the characters in the pictures.

Heading back toward the north, the visitor leaves behind the lush vegetation and paddy fields stretching as far as the eye can see, so typical of the landscape in the south. Little by little, the atmosphere changes radically. Central China is part of the so-called "river region" which opens up between the country's two main waterways, the Yangtze or Blue River, to the south, and the Huanghe or Yellow River, to the north. The Huanghe's alluvial plain lies in the north of Anhui province, the provinces of Henan and Hebei and the western part of Shandong. It is particularly fertile thanks to the loess, the silt yellow sand that the rivers and winds bring southeast from the plateaux in the northeast and the Gobi Desert. This place gave rise to a legend about a people, the Chinese people, created from the clay of the Yellow River, which gave

recent Chinese history. It was in 1935 that at Yan'an in Shaanxi the Long March (*changzeng*) ended, with the arrival of around 8000 survivors of the 100,000 militants who had set off. The march had begun in the south, far away in Jiangxi, at the end of the previous year; with this forced 7440-mile (12,000-km) march to the north, the Communists sought to avoid encirclement by the Guomindang forces, led by Jiang Jieshi (Chiang Kai-shek). And it was also in Yan'an, on the border with the areas under Nationalist control, that the Communist headquarters were set up the following decade.

Shaanxi sits at the crossroads between the routes leading from east to west, on one side, and the north-south axis on the other. Thanks to their strategic position between eastern and western China, this province and Shanxi were among the first areas to come into contact with Buddhism when it reached the country.

China's artistic heritage was strongly influenced by this religion, and colossal works were created in its name, such as the imposing rock sculpture complexes; of all the Buddhist artistic masterpieces in China, these have remained in the best condition, defying time, invasions and wars. In the north of Shanxi, at Datong, not far from the capital Taiyuan, is the Yungang rock complex. It stretches for almost

them their skin tone. To the west of Henan and Hebei provinces are two provinces with curiously similar names: Shanxi, west of the Taihang mountains, and farther north, Shaanxi, on the border with Gansu and Ningxia Hui.

The Fenhe, a tributary of the Yellow River, crosses Shanxi province from north to south,; while another of the large river's tributaries, the Wei, crosses Shaanxi province from west to east, forming a fertile valley that was one of the key locations for the development of Chinese civilization. In fact, Shaanxi contains traces of some of the most ancient settlements, and the capitals of over ten dynasties were located at the site of what is now Xi'an, the provincial capital. Again in the 20th century, this province became the backdrop to one of the symbolic moments of

a mile from east to west and consists of 53 caves cut out of the sandstone rock face on the southern face of Mt. Wuzhou. Here, over 50,000 sacred images were carved out of the rock, including Buddhas, bodhisattvas, apsaras (heavenly dancers depicted as flying creatures), monks, believers and disciples of the Enlightened One. This place of worship, which is close to the border with Inner Mongolia, was one of the most important of those associated with Buddhism. It was built between around 460 and 490 A.C. under the Tuobas, an ethnic group of Turkic origin that founded the Northern Wei dynasty (386-535). The foreign influx from India and central Asia can be seen clearly in the sculptures at Yungang, where artists flocked from both abroad and from the Dunhuang area in Gansu province.

Another important religious center in the east of the Shanxi province is Wutaishan ("the mountain of five terraces") in the Taihang range, which takes its name from its distinctive five peaks with flat, wide summits. This has been an important place for Buddhist worship ever since the Tang era, when some of its temples were built – they are the oldest wooden buildings in the country. At that time, it became one of the main centers for the diffusion of the new religion, with thousands of monks working on the translation of classic Buddhist texts. As the visitor moves gradually northward across these provinces toward Mongolia, the landscape changes quite drastically and the air becomes different. Shaanxi, for example, is divided by natural barriers into three distinct areas, with very different climates. In the southern part is the mountainous Qinba region, which separates the Yangtze basin to the south from the Huanghe basin to the north. It consists of the Qinling and Dabashan ranges, which together enclose the Hanshui valley, where the Hanzhong depression, an area with a northern subtropical climate, has landscapes reminiscent of southern China. In the center is the Guanzhong plain, a fertile area that is particularly suitable for cultivation due to its

warm, temperate climate. Beyond Xi'an, moving north, visitors arrive at the northern Shaanxi plateau, in the center of the Loess region, an area formed of lime and loess deposits and offering a temperate climate. The Chinese call it Huangtu Gaoyuan ("tableland of yellow earth"). On this arid plateau, which was once flat, rivers have eroded the soil and furrowed deep canyons. Humans then changed the environment even further, terracing the hills to exploit as best they could this arid, inhospitable land, fought over inch by inch by the farmers. The rough slopes, terraced and pierced by caves that are often used as homes, create some harsh, striking scenery.

To the north, beyond the Great Wall, lies the endless plateau of Inner Mongolia, an autonomous region that is four times the size of Italy. Here

– in addition to mountains, steppes and forests – is the Gobi Desert; it is populated by camels, brown bears, gazelles, snow leopards and wolves. It has a continental climate with long, cold winters and short summers. To the west, Inner Mongolia extends as far as the Beishan mountain range, beyond which is the province of Xinjiang. In the east, the plateau borders on the provinces of Liaoning, Jilin and Heilongjiang. Most of Hunan ("south of the river") is indeed situated south of the Huanghe. This province has a wealth of archaeological sites, and is considered the cradle of Chinese civilization. It was the seat of various capitals and has some important artistic heritage. According to tradition, the first Buddhist temple in China was built in the city of Luoyang, the capital of several early dynasties. A few miles from Luoyang, beyond the muddy waters of the Yihe (a tributary of the Yellow River), an imposing image of the Buddha can be made out through the early morning mist. This is the Vairocana of the Fengxian temple; standing 56 ft (17 m) tall, it is the masterpiece of a group carved into the limestone wall between 672 and 675, during the Tang era. This immense work is just one some 100,000 images scattered over 2345 caves and niches, carved out over almost three centuries (between the 5th and 8th centuries A.D.). The Buddhist sculpture complex of Longmen, which was built with the labor of millions of people, is the most intricate in the whole of Asia. Kaifeng, in the north of the province, was also the capital for various dynasties; but its greatest period of glory was under the Northern Song dynasty and the Jin. It is a pleasant place, which maintains the atmosphere of the Chinese

103 **TOP** The Great Wall is a serpent of clay bricks over 6,000 kilometres long, armed with thousands of watchtowers. During the Qin dynasty in the 3rd century B.C., various blocks that already existed were joined together again, to form the first true Great Wall; it served as a bulwark against the periodic invasions of nomads who came down into the Middle Kingdom from the Mongolian and Siberian steppes

103 **BOTTOM** Along the lower course of the Ejin Nur, in Inner Mongolia, are the ruins of Iji Nai, the ancient capital of the Western Xia, which stood on the Silk Route. This dynasty was founded in 1038 by a tribe of Tanguts, and later fell under the Mongol attacks of 1227.

cities of old, especially in the area within the ancient city walls; it has done so despite all the natural disasters caused by the violence of the nearby Huanghe, and the devastation wrought by wars and invasions over its three thousand years of history. The municipalities of Beijing and Tianjin are wedged into the nearby province of Hebei, "north of the river" (meaning the Huanghe, of course); the latter of the two cities is full of lingering memories of its cosmopolitan past, when Japanese, Russians and Europeans lived side by side.

North-east, over the Great Wall, Chengde (Jehol) hosts the summer residence built on the mountains, to escape the torrid heat of the capital, by the emperors of the Qing dynasty between 1703 and 1792. A walk around the largest imperial garden in China, enclosed by a wall over 6 miles (10 km) long, leads to over 110 buildings. These include noble residences, administrative buildings and temples, in a microcosm made up of footbridges, rocks, terraces and inscriptions distributed seemingly at random, in the Chinese style. In these green surroundings, with parks and woods, there is the lakeshore along which stand towers, pavilions and pagodas with magic-sounding names. A vaguely exotic air envelops the Eight Exterior Temples, a group of monasteries and Buddhist sanctuaries outside the walls which display a harmonious combination of various architectural styles, from Tibet and Mongolia but also from central China. In fact, some of the buildings in this summer residence were copied from originals all over the country, especially in the border areas; it is as though, in this place for leisure and relaxation, the sovereigns wished to reproduce the signs of their power in the world, with the intention of glorifying their policy of religious and political unification between the various nationalities. The Putuo Zongcheng, or Little Potala, for example, is a copy of the one in Lhasa, while the Xumi Fushouzhimiao (or Monastery of Happiness and Longevity of Mt. Sumeru) is an imitation of the Tibetan monastery of Tashilhunpo in Shigatse, although it has some details in the typical Han style. Meanwhile the Xuguang, a round pavilion in the Pule (Temple of Universal Joy), is inspired by the Tiantan, the Temple of Heaven, in the capital. Similarly, various scenes and gardens were recreated to resemble specific landscapes in particular areas of the Celestial Empire.

The nearby municipality of Beijing contains some of the best preserved – but also most tourist-ridden – sections of the Great Wall. It has come to symbolize the country and is perhaps the best example of the hard work and perseverance of the Chinese people. The first parts of the wall were built during the time of the Warring States, in about the 5th to 6th centuries B.C., by the principalities of Qin, Zhao and Yan to stop the sporadic invasions by hordes of nomads from the Mongolian and Siberian steppes. The various sections were then joined together during the Qin dynasty in the 3rd century B.C., when the first true Great Wall was created, which over the centuries had its periods of maintenance and neglect and later ended up is great disrepair. Hongwu (1368-98), the first emperor of the Ming dynasty, restored it to a useful role by reuniting the various sections – which differed in their structure and materials – into one single defense bulwark over 3720 miles (6000 km) long, armed with thousands of watchtowers. It extended from the Gulf of Liaodong, on the border with what is now North Korea, as far as the border with the vast deserts of Xinjiang. This belt of wall, which is between 23 and 26.4 ft (7 and 8 m) tall and on average, about 20 ft (6 m) wide, separates the Gobi Desert from the fertile Chinese plain. Although the Great Wall was a valid defense system against the ordinary invasions that took place along the border, in actual fact it was never able to block the more serious invasions to which China fell victim, especially when the wall itself was left to deteriorate. This, then, was an insuperable bulwark on paper only; in the 12th century, for example, it was unable to stop Genghis Khan's Mongol army.

Farther north, past the Great Wall, east of the Hebei province, lie Liaoning, Jilin and Heilongjiang, the three provinces that make up the Dongbei (the "northeast"); this used to be Manchuria, from where the founders of China's last final dynasty came. The Heilongjiang – "Black Dragon River," as the Chinese call the Amur – is in China's the northernmost province, where in winter temperatures fall to as low as -20° C. Just south of here, on the Yellow Sea, the Shandong province provides evidence of the pure Chinese spirit. The Taishan, the most sacred of the Taoist mountains, is in this province. And also here, in Qufu, in what used to be the principality of Lu in the time of the Warring States, is where Confucius was born (551-479 B.C.); this great thinker conditioned the course of Chinese history. A visit to the master's birthplace, where some of the most classic Confucian temples in China are to be found, is the ideal way to conclude this journey across the Middle Kingdom. (M.M. and F.R.)

104-105 A FARMER LEADS
TWO WATER BUFFALOES, AGAINST
THE BACKDROP OF THE GUILIN
HILLS (GUANGXI), A CHAIN OF
UPRIGHT LIMESTONE
FORMATIONS THAT HAVE BEEN
CARVED INTO BIZARRE SHAPES
BY EROSION.

THE HEART OF THE GIANT | 105

106-107 In the southern part of the course of the Lijiang, the river Li (Guangxi), at dusk men fish in the traditional way, using a cormorant, on boats lit by lanterns.

107 As this picture shows, fishing with cormorants, when seen together with the pointed silhouettes of the mountains encircling the horizon of the river Li, makes this region particularly spectacular.

108-109 THIS PHOTOGRAPH, WHICH SHOWS SEVERAL FISHING BOATS WITH CORMORANTS, WAS TAKEN AT DAWN, A MAGIC MOMENT AMONG THE WATER AND THE SHARP PEAKS OF GUANGXI, ONE OF THE MOST EXTRAORDINARY LANDSCAPES IN CHINA.

110-111 In several areas of the southern province of Guangxi, the Zhuang ethnic group has dug spectacular rice terraces into the hills.

112-113 IN 1999, THE WUYI MOUNTAINS IN THE NORTH-EAST OF FUJIAN WERE PLACED ON THE UNESCO WORLD HERITAGE LIST.

114-115 THE SCENIC AREA OF WULINGYUAN, IN THE NORTH-WEST OF HUNAN, IS MADE UP OF 3,100 QUARTZITE PINNACLES THAT ARE UP TO 400 METRES HIGH.

116-117 In the north-western province of Gansu, at Laolongwan ("Old Dragon Bay"), where the Yellow River meets the Great Wall, there is a Stone Forest that covers an area of ten square kilometres.

117 The Stone Forest of the Yellow River is made up of yellowish gravel sedimentations; this spectacular geological rarity was formed four million years ago, but its remote position meant that it was only discovered in 1990.

118-119 Mount Huashan (2,200 metres) is 120 kilometres east of Xi'an, in the northern province of Shaanxi; seen from above, it looks like a five-petalled flower.

120-121 Mount Tai, or Taishan, is in the eastern province of Shandong, and is the most important of the five sacred mountains of Taoism.

THE CITIES OF TOMORROW

BEIJING
NEW BEIJING GREAT OLYMPICS
北京2008年奥运会申办委员会 Beijing 2008 Olympic Games Bid Committee

122 **CLOCKWISE FROM LEFT** A COLOURFUL MARKET IN CANTON; ONE OF THE MANY COLONIAL-STYLE BUILDINGS IN MACAU; POSTER FOR THE BEIJING 2008 OLYMPICS; THE JINGMAO, IN SHANGHAI, THE TALLEST BUILDING IN CHINA AND THE SECOND TALLEST IN ASIA, ON THE EASTERN BANK OF THE HUANGPU.

123 THE FUTURISTIC SKYSCRAPER OF THE BANK OF CHINA WITH ITS TWO LONG ANTENNAE TOWERS OVER THE OTHER BUILDINGS THAT STAND ON THE BAY OF HONG KONG.

124 IN THE CITY OF HANGZHOU, CAPITAL OF THE DENSELY INHABITED ZHEJIANG PROVINCE, THE XIHU, OR WESTERN LAKE, REFLECTS THE REDDISH LIGHT OF THE SUNSET.

125 **LEFT AND RIGHT** WHILE CANTON DRESSES UP COLOURFULLY FOR FESTIVALS, BY NIGHT MACAU LIGHTS UP WITH VIVID NEON LIGHTS TO ATTRACT CLIENTS TO THE CASINOS.

THE CITIES OF TOMORROW

A lot of water has passed under the bridges of Chinese cities since Marco Polo admiringly described their wealth and majesty in his book of travels. Who knows what he would think today if he could visit the same places: Sindifu, today called Chengdu, or Quegianfu, which is now Xi'an, "which in ancient times was a good and powerful kingdom," as he wrote. Or cold Khanbaliq with its twelve gates, where Kublai Khan had his palace: today it is the nation's capital, congested with a sea of traffic that flows constantly through its vast multi-lane highways. It has been invaded by skyscrapers that are spreading everywhere, replacing the traditional houses with courtyards and the *hutong*, the alleyways of old Peking. But more than any other, Polo loved the magical city of Quinsai, where the Grand Khan sent him several times to collect taxes. Today, the city is called Hangzhou, and is still there with its pretty West Lake, the *joie de vivre* of its citizens and its culinary delights. Today, it is one of the favorite destinations for Chinese tourists, but little remains of its glorious past: many buildings and works of art were destroyed in 1861 during the Taiping revolt, and again one hundred years later by the Cultural Revolution's Red Guards. Even though only a few old buildings and pagodas remain, Hangzhou still has great charm and an extraordinary atmosphere, thanks to its lake. Accompanied by birdsong, a white mist rises each morning over its water, which is always crossed by flights of geese. Its three islands are hermitages, far from the frenzy of modern China. Marco Polo, who visited Hangzhou when it was at its pinnacle and had almost two million inhabitants, loved it immensely and described it as the "most splendid" city; he describes Suzhou, an ancient city built on a canal network just farther north, was "large and noble." Both cities certainly deserve the reputation they have

from an ancient Chinese saying, which says, "In the sky there is paradise, on earth Hangzhou and Suzhou." It is curious that the Venetian traveler preferred the former, because Suzhou — with its criss-cross of waterways and the infinity of bridges above them — must have reminded the Polo family of their own city. Over three hundred years after the Venetian's journey, the Jesuit Daniello Bartoli, while processing and organizing the information contained in the reports sent by missionaries in the Far East, asserted that "the walled cities, if counted altogether, including the large, the medium and the small ones, number over fifteen hundred... The way the cities are, in terms of design, is almost the same in all of them: that is, arranged in a square, surrounded by deep ditches, closed in by large embankments circled by very high walls, many in rough stone, most in brick." Indeed, until the Revolution and the declaration of the Republic in 1949, the typical Chinese city had a quadrangular form, a rectangle with gates that opened in the middle of each side of the imposing walls, which sometimes had battlements. Perfectly orientated, the city was crossed by two main streets which intersected in the center. The thick wall surrounding the city itself separated two worlds, somehow confirming the contrast between urban life and the country. Still today, much of the population — around 60 percent — lives in rural areas, and China is still an agricultural country, despite the rapid industrialization of recent decades and the astounding growth and modernity of its giant urban centers, to which millions of people flock from the countryside. Indeed, from around the 1950s, places which for centuries had been political-administrative or trading centers have gradually become industrial centers capable of attracting millions of workers from the rural areas. All over the country, especially in the cities in the

126 ANCIENT AND NEW CUSTOMS LIVE SIDE BY SIDE IN CANTON AS THEY DO IN MANY CHINESE CITIES: A WOMAN HOLDING A LIVE CHICKEN WALKS PAST A HUGE BILLBOARD.

127 CANTON, KNOWN IN CHINA AS GUANGZHOU, HAS A FUTURISTIC SKYLINE TRACED OUT BY SKYSCRAPERS, TOWERED OVER BY THE CITIC PLAZA TOWERS, IN THE CENTRE.

128-129 ALTHOUGH IT IS ONE OF THE OLDEST CHINESE CITIES, CANTON HAS A VERY MODERN APPEARANCE. AS CAN BE SEEN HERE, ITS HORIZON IS DOMINATED BY RECENTLY BUILT BUILDINGS AND STRUCTURES.

delta of the Yangtze and the Pearl River, urban areas are expanding vastly to accommodate those who move from the country to the city. These cities are marked by the race toward well-being, the spreading of wealth, the birth of new social and cultural phenomena; this is a contrast to the harsh reality and relative poverty of the countryside, where living conditions are often unchanged and work in the fields is still done almost entirely manually, especially by women. China, which is the most populated country in the world with its 1.3 billion inhabitants, is experiencing a frenzied rush toward urbanization. Cities have become the key to modernizing and enriching a nation that, in the last ten years, has shown the largest growth rate in history. The rate of urbanization is now around 30 percent. There are agglomerates of a staggering size: the municipality of Shanghai now exceeds twenty million inhabitants, and the population of Chongqing, the largest port on the Yangtze river, is the biggest in the world, at over 31 million. Beijing has reached the 15 million mark, of which around 11.5 million live there permanently, while Tianjin has a population of about 10 million. Chengdu and Canton have about 10 million inhabitants and several other cities have a population in excess of 5 million: Nanjing, Hangzhou, Suzhou, Xi'an and Wuhan are just some of them. In the category between 1 and 5 million inhabitants there are around 40 cities, some of which have names that are practically unheard of in the rest of the world. Beijing, and to a greater extent Shanghai, have turned into futuristic megalopolises that are able to challenge the former technological capital of Hong Kong in terms of development and modernity. They are also capable of throwing down the gauntlet – when it comes to growth rate, efficiency of transport and modernity of infrastructure – to the most celebrated cities in the West. The mania for construction that accompanies this unstoppable development of the urban centers is one of the first things that the visitor notices in any Chinese city. Already in the 1980s, buildings could be seen sprouting up everywhere, and it was normal to see construction workers at night, guided by searchlights, on seemingly shaky

bamboo scaffolding; one would realize that a building had visibly doubled or tripled in height in the space of a few weeks. Millions of new buildings have been built in recent decades, corroding the historic image and layout of many cities. This is also why some movements are starting up in China that aim to promote traditional architecture, against the general trend of mechanically and routinely using Western-style shapes and stereotypes. Among the factories, skyscrapers, super-fast transport and huge shopping centers, a lot of big cities still contain the traces of many imperial dynasties and the roots of Chinese culture. Including Beijing, Shanghai and Hong Kong there are around ten cities that represent this magical mix between past, present and future. Canton, for example, the capital of Guangdong province, in the Pearl River delta: known in China as Guangzhou, it was one of the first cities to open up to the free market, and is now one of the richest in China, and the third city in historical importance after Beijing and Shanghai. It did not host imperial dynasties like Nanjing and Xi'an did, but it was the first port that the Celestial Empire opened to the world. For centuries it was a hub for trading between China, the Middle East and Southeast Asia, run first by the Arabs and later by the Portuguese. Today, Canton is a megalopolis of 10 million citizens. The city's commercial and cultural dynamism (it has many artists and with the rockstar Wang Lei it has become the capital of the Chinese 'angry music' scene) means that it is known as the city in which there is more to do than to see. Ancient temples still stand among the skyscrapers, like the Buddhist one in Guangxiao dedicated to filial piety; it was founded in the 4th century A.D. but its buildings date from later. Here, according to tradition, Hui Neng (638-713), the founder of the *chan* Buddhist school (Japanese Zen) is supposed to have done his novitiate. There is also the Buddhist Liurongsi, ("Temple of the Six Banyans") which is extremely ancient and most of which dates from the 11th century. Inside it there is a temple dedicated to Guanyin, bodhisattva of Compassion, and the octagonal Huata ("Flower Pagoda") which is the tallest in the city.

Portugal was responsible for creating a trading base on the coast, not far from Canton, where Macau prospered. With its old Portuguese houses, nowadays it has the air of the last outpost of the East Indias Company. A Lusitanian colony until 1557, for centuries this was Lisbon's commercial base in the Far East. From its port, silk, porcelain and spices reached Europe, India and Brazil: the cornerstones of an empire built on geographical discoveries and consolidated through trading. Macau was returned to Beijing in 1999 with a special statue for its 450,000 inhabitants, similar to that drawn up for Hong Kong (it guarantees fifty years of political and economic autonomy). It was the longest-lasting colony in Asia: the Portuguese flag flew here for 442 years. Situated on a peninsula at the mouth of the Pearl River, it covers a surface area of just 16 square kilometres, including the islands of Taipa and Coloane, which are linked to the continent by long bridges.

Nowadays it appears to be a crossroads between China and the West, between its colonial past and the high technology of its new international airport.

The glass, steel and cement skyscrapers overshadow baroque churches, while at Chinese New Year, multicoloured dragons with pyrotechnic tails made of bangers invade the streets, as do processions to celebrate the anniversary of the apparition of Our Lady of Fatima. The two cultures have lived side by side without friction, but basically ignoring each other. A typical example is the story behind the baroque cathedral of São Paulo, which is the most beautiful monument to Christianity to be found in the Far East. It was built without taking into account the rules of *fengshui*, the geomantic theory which determines the best place in which to construct a building. First destroyed by fire, and then again by a typhoon, it was never rebuilt. High up at the top of a flight of steps, it has been reduced to a mere façade, framed by the sky. So the Catholics, who make up three percent of the population, pray at the church of São Domingo: a baroque jewel with courtyards lined with *azulejos,* the traditional Portuguese tiles. The multicultural vocation resurfaces in restaurants where Portuguese, Chinese, Indian and African ingredients are mixed. And the gambling that took place in the chaotic old town has been moved into the big hotels, where it is advertised by large neon signs. Casinos open twenty-four hours a day feed the city's fever, together with dog and horse racing. The little Las Vegas of the East, Macau is destined to become the playground of Southern China.

The huge city of Chengdu, capital of populous Sichuan province, is also full of contradictions. It is a chaotic flowering of skyscrapers, shopping centers and road junctions, as well as the location of the colorful Qingshiqiao market; this visual and olfactory plunge into the Far East has spices, all sorts of vegetables, ceramics, traditional fabrics, household goods, caged birds, bamboo objects, plants and exotic flowers, street food and butchers of the most bizarre animals, from yaks to toads and snakes. The city of Chongqing is an autonomous municipality in the east of Sichuan, and is the country's largest river harbor, at the confluence of the Yangtze,

To defend it, he built a brick wall around the city, 23 ft (7 m) thick and 40 ft (12 m) high, with a perimeter of 20.5 miles (33 km). This was the longest city wall in the world, with thirteen entry gates. Two of the main gates have survived, together with two thirds of the city wall. Today, Nanjing is a fast-expanding industrial city, with industrial companies producing textiles, food, iron and steel, metal, mechanics, chemicals and cement. Its two-level steel bridge that spans the Yangtze is the symbol of Chinese independence and modernity; in fact, the Chinese completed it 1968, after Russian engineers had abandoned the project for political reasons. Farther north is

Zhengzhou, the capital of Henan province; it is an immense modern city with a population of over 6 million. It is a network of straight avenues, overlooked by a soaring forest of skyscrapers; it contains some of the largest shopping centers in China, as well as extraordinary archaeological remains and fascinating historical and science museums, such as the Henan Museum, the fourth largest in China, and the brand-new Museum of Science and Technology. Finally, there is Xi'an; this is

Jialing and Fujiang rivers; it is the industrial fulcrum of western China as well as the main center of attraction for the mass of country people escaping from rural life. Its resistant urban landscape, with steep rises and sharp drops, makes this the only Chinese city without bicycles. On the banks of the Jialing river stands the old quarter of Ciqikou, which has survived the influence of modernity; this area still has wooden houses, alleyways, courtyards shared by several families with kitchens under the arcades and a huge number of tea houses where men and women challenge each other to games of cards or mah-jong.

Continuing along the Yangtze, the visitor come to Nanjing, the first capital of the Ming dynasty (1368-1644), where all the gravity of its imperial past can be felt; in fact, Nanjing means "capital of the south." During the thirty years that he reigned, Hongwu, the dynasty's first emperor, turned Nanjing into the most beautiful, wealthy and secure city in China.

the capital of Shaanxi, a cold province in central-northern China, with 7 million inhabitant. Xi'an was the capital of the great Qin, Sui and Tang empires, dynasties which left encircling that enclose the old city. Some 25 miles (40 km) away is the mausoleum of the First Emperor, Shi Huangdi; this is the most intriguing necropolis in the world, as well as the most visited archaeological excavation in China. UNESCO has declared it a World Heritage site, and the Terracotta Army that protected the deceased emperor is considered to the greatest masterpiece of Chinese plastic arts. In the centuries that followed, Xi'an became the starting point of the Silk Route, the caravan route that passed through many cities in western China before reaching Central Asia and Europe. For two thousand years it was the crossroads of peoples and goods from the provinces of the Far East and the steppes of Central Asia; today it is one of the most popular tourist sites in the country. (M.M.)

136-137 The main square of Chengdu is dominated by a giant statue of Mao Zedong, which contrasts with the bright neon of the advertisements on the exhibition building.

138-139 Situated at the confluence of three rivers, Chongqing is the largest municipality in the world, with 32 million inhabitants, as well as the symbol of the race towards urbanization in China.

140-141 Nanjing, located on the Yangzi, was the cradle of the Ming dynasty. The southern part of the city is crossed by a 3-mile stretch of the Qinhuai. A lively district dotted with shops and restaurants developed along the riverbanks between the 14th and the 20th century.

142-143 The picture shows the copy of a statue from the Terracotta Army and a bicycle parked in an alley in old Xi'an, where the ancient quarters are held in by a series of imposing walls.

144-145 The Terracotta Army in Xi'an is the legacy of a sovereign who was so powerful that he could have his mausoleum protected by an army of thousands of life-size men, made one by one out of terracotta, each with a different posture, expression and facial features.

146 The geometric regularity of the Forbidden City can be seen clearly in this view from above, taken from the Tian'anmen Square side; it shows the main pavilions perfectly aligned along the central axis.

147 FROM LEFT A stone stele with inscriptions in the Summer Palace in Beijing; an enormous "Fo dog" or dog of Buddha, in golden bronze in the Forbidden City; one of the groups of sculptures that surround Mao's mausoleum.

BEIJING
CAPITAL OF THE EMPIRE

The capital is a huge building site, a "work in progress" toward the future. Modernity is advancing and the *hutong*, the traditional alley of Beijing, is disappearing. In 2000 these alleys covered only a third of the city; today, probably just over one-fifth. It is a shame, as the *hutong* is the memory, the soul, of an extremely ancient country. They are made up of the typical *siheyuan*, grey houses with inner courtyards on just one level, as no building was permitted to be as tall as the imperial palaces. These narrow streets are always crowded with people, stalls, shops, women cooking, children playing and bamboo cages for crickets or songbirds. The idea of "out with the old" is nothing new in China, where a popular song says "We have five thousand years of history, but a very youthful smile"; where, for millennia, the imperial dynasties succeeded each other, destroying the buildings that represented the power of the previous rulers. It was Mao who brought the capital back here in 1949, after the victory of the revolution, silencing the claims of Xi'an, Canton and Nanjing. Beijing certainly has all

the features of a capital city. The difference with Shanghai is striking: while the latter is cheerful and tolerant, Beijing is serious, pragmatic and slightly arrogant. Its inhabitants are harder people, forged by a continental climate with winter temperatures of -15°C, and summers at over 40°C, and by their proximity to the centers of power. They are proud, northern Chinese people, somewhat haughty, and evidently feel a sense of superiority over their compatriots in the southern regions.

The heart of Beijing is Tian'anmen Square, the "Gate to Heavenly Peace." It has always been the center of power, in imperial China and during Maoist times, and it still is, now that real socialism has teamed up with the free market in a frenetic scramble toward modernity. It is a vast esplanade which can hold over a million people, and is thought to be the largest square in the world, with a surface area of almost 1000 acres (400 hectares). Mao Zedong had it laid out in the early 1950s, at the cost of demolishing one of the areas that best represented traditional Beijing architecture. This

147 BOTTOM Wangfujing is Beijing's commercial street, its gleaming showcase with luxury restaurants, boutiques, shopping centres, discos and internet cafés. The yuppie heart of the city into which Beijing's inhabitants pour their consumerist desires.

was the period when modernization and communist rationalism began, when the Communist Party decided to tear down the city walls to make way for a ring road. In that time of enormous restraints, following decades of wars, the Central Committee wanted to occupy the Forbidden City. Mao did not allow this to happen, saying that he was not a new emperor: by doing so, he preserved one of the most important Chinese monuments. Today, the "Great Helmsman" lies in the mausoleum dedicated to him in the center of the square, not far from the obelisk dedicated to the People's Heroes.

forest of cubes and rectangular blocks that typify its architecture.

On the north side of Tian'anmen Square, the gate of the same name with its enormous, classic portrait of Mao leads to the Forbidden City, so called because it was the domain of the court and the people were not granted access. This vast complex with its tens of palaces, pavilions and temples, containing 9000 rooms altogether, is a magnificent reminder of imperial China. It was built in the 15th century when the emperors of the Ming dynasty (1368-1644) transferred their residence here from Nanjing; Beijing, in fact, means "northern capital." The best overall view of this extraordinary architectural complex, which provides an idea of its impressiveness and rigorous geometry, is to be had from the artificial "Coal Hill" in the adjacent Jingshan park, at the northern tip of the central north-south axis that crosses the Forbidden City. A visit takes one around courtyards and buildings with roofs embellished with figures of mythical animals that protect

Tian'anmen Square is surrounded by buildings and monuments. To the east it is flanked by the Palace Museum, which houses the renovated Museum of Chinese History with its extraordinary collection of bronzes and ceramics; facing it to the west is the National People's Assembly. Next to this vast building stands the new Beijing Opera House, the huge National Theater designed by the French architect Paul Andreu; this is the capital's most futuristic, spectacular building: a gigantic bubble covered in titanium and surrounded by pools of water. This is the only rounded building, along with the Temple of Heaven farther south, in a city that is otherwise almost obsessively squared off: from the chessboard of straight roads with right-angled cross roads that make up the city's layout, to the

against evil spirits, in a jubilation of colors: red, the symbol of good fortune, luck and success; yellow, the color of the earth and the emperor; green, which evokes the idea of rebirth; blue, which is associated with immortality. Beyond the threshold of the pavilions, in the semi-darkness of the interiors, furniture, sculptures and objects can be made out which belonged to the regal inhabitants of this complex, and to their wives and concubines.

Following the fortunes of one of these, the Empress Cixi, leads us to Beijing's other imperial wonder, the Summer Palace: about 12.5 miles (20 km) from the current city center, where the ancient summer residence stood before the British destroyed it during the second Opium War. Cixi had this majestic residence built; it came to symbolize her unbridled ambition. The daughter of a low-ranking civil servant, she became the mistress of the Emperor Wenzong at the age of 17. She then rose in the ranks until she reached her ultimate goal, that of supreme power: after the Emperor's death in 1861 she became the de facto ruler until she died in 1908. The Summer Palace was a whim on which she squandered huge amounts of money that had been set aside for defense; some historians attribute the consequent fall of the Qing dynasty (1644-1912) to her decision. The steam boat with a stone wheel, set up as a reception hall, met with particular disapproval; it can still be admired today on the banks of Lake Kunming. The Palace is divided into poetically-named pavilions, courtyards, bridges and gardens: the Hall of Joy and Longevity, the Garden of Virtue and Harmony, the Pagoda of Buddhist Fragrance, the Hall in which to listen to the nightingale's song. There are also staircases and parades, such as the "Long Corridor," a splendidly painted covered wooden gallery, 2400 ft (728 m) long.

A few steps from the Forbidden City is Wangfujing, Beijing's glittering

showcase, a street with luxury restaurants, boutiques, shopping malls, discos and internet cafés. This is the yuppie soul of the city, where crowds of Chinese buy cashmere sweaters, clothes and lengths of silk, raincoats in every color, pearls, jade necklaces, porcelain, fine teas and, in particular, technological gadgets. This is the best-known commercial area in a city that is 62 miles (100 km) from side to side and that is undergoing some very major changes. The center was completely cleaned up in 1999 for the 50th-year anniversary of the People's Republic. But Beijing had already been in ferment for some years. Under a thick sky, darkened by dust and sand from the Gobi desert, new tree-lined arteries with four, five, even six lanes in each direction ripped through the city's ancient

quarters. The horizon filled up with hundreds of skyscrapers topped with traditional-style roofs, luxury hotels and vast shopping centers, all fed by an unprecedented economic boom. Bicycles, which once symbolized Maoist China, were confined to the side-roads to make way for an army of taxis and for the cars produced by joint ventures between Chinese and Western companies.

But the charm of old China can still be felt in some areas. In Dachilan, for example, a bustling shopping street a few minutes from Tian'anmen square: this is the street of the traditional silk emporiums, of the tea houses and old fashioned pharmacies. Or in Liulichang, the antiques bazaar which has been overrun by tourists for years now, with its old wooden houses bursting with antique furniture, porcelain and works of art mixed up with fakes and junk, and its shops selling brushes, ink, sketchpads and fine paper for calligraphy. Or the Temple of Heaven, which stands out for its circular building; it is located at the southern end of the north-south axis that extends with perfect geometry from the Forbidden City and used to be paraded down by the emperor during official ceremonies. Not forgetting the ancient Temple of the Lama, the most picturesque of all, with its frescoes, fabrics and excellent woodwork, which housed Mongolian and Tibetan monks from the 18th century onward. (M.M.)

152-153 THIS IMAGE WAS TAKEN IN FRONT OF THE ONE OF THE PAVILIONS OF THE FORBIDDEN CITY; IT WAS BUILT IN A TRIUMPH OF COLOURS, ESPECIALLY GOLD AND RED, WHICH SYMBOLISE LAND AND SUCCESS FOR THE CHINESE, AND GREEN AND BLUE, WHICH SYMBOLISE GOOD LUCK FOR THE FUTURE AND REBIRTH.

154-155 A WOMAN STRIDES PAST LARGE CHARACTERS WRITTEN IN RELIEF ON A WALL, AS SHE TALKS ON HER MOBILE PHONE. THIS IS THE SYMBOL OF A CHINA THAT IS RACING RAPIDLY TOWARDS THE FUTURE, WHILE NEVER FORGETTING ITS GREAT PAST.

156-157 The buildings at Dongfang Plaza house the Urban and Environmental Science faculty of Beijing University, as well as a cultural centre for studies on the discovery of archaeological sites from the Palaeolithic era.

157 As this image shows, the streets of Beijing are equipped with a dense network of phone booths, showing one of the many aspects of the modernisation that is underway in the Chinese capital.

158-159 A man looks at the portraits of Mao Zedong and other communist leaders in a shop window in Beijing. Despite the great changes that are taking place in China, the figure of the Great Helmsman has never been questioned.

160-161 This photo shows the night time crowd in Wangfujing, where Beijing's inhabitants flock to buy cashmere sweaters, garments and reams of silk, pearls, jade necklaces, porcelain, fine teas, but above all technological gadgets.

161 The Kerry Centre is a modern luxury hotel in the Chaoyang district, which is the area of Beijing made up of skyscrapers; it has become the hub of diplomatic, commercial and financial activity in the Chinese capital.

SHANGHAI

AN EASTERN METROPOLIS

At six in the morning on Shanghai's Bund, the main thoroughfare that runs along the River Huangpu, women of all ages turn gracefully in the fan dance, the gentlest form of expression linked to martial arts. They move elegantly amid the traffic, a terrace of 1920s buildings, and against a horizon dominated by the futuristic Pudong skyline. They hover lightly next to couples waltzing to the rhythm of croaking tape recorders, among acrobats on rollerblades and old people practising tai chi exercises or flying kites. All that remains of the old Chinese customs takes place at dawn. Then it is time to go to work in the offices of Pudong, between the sci-fi Oriental East Pearl TV & Radio Tower, a cement tower 1544 ft (468 m) high, the Barcelo conference center with its auditorium enclosed in a huge glass bubble, or the Customs Authority's skyscraper, topped with a sort of flying saucer with fluorescent ideograms. Or time to go to the factories, which have sprung up in their thousands in the endless suburbs and countless satellite towns. Or perhaps in one of the many taxis and buses that swarm through the tunnels under the river or along the network of motorways and intersections that link up the tentacles of a megalopolis with 17 million inhabitants, not counting the fluctuating population of at least 3 million temporary workers. Or then again, to work in the largest shopping mall on earth, or in the shops, markets and department stores of Nanjinglu, the central pedestrian shopping street which is lit up by a forest of neon signs that would put New York to shame. The street is overflowing with goods, is polished by an army of street sweepers, brightened up by dancers and musicians, and kept in order by giant screens and digital displays that dictate the rules of conduct. This is the most visible symbol of a country in frenetic pursuit of well-being. These are the most eloquent places in the city that is growing and changing more quickly than any other in the world; the megalopolis that best represents China's ambition as a world superpower. Shanghai is the bustling laboratory of the China of tomorrow, a preview of the advanced 21st century.

163 TOP LEFT AND RIGHT These pictures show the modern soul of Shanghai: left, the coloured neon signs of a club in Huaihai Road; right, a panoramic view of the city centre.

163 BOTTOM In this picturesque image, bicycles trace out faint designs on the street of one of the bridges of Shanghai, throwing down their shadows in the light of the sunset.

The city is a non-stop building site, as well as being the only one in the world that has more than 2000 skyscrapers; another 400 are already under construction. This ultra-modern metropolis, colorful, lively and dynamic, rivals Tokyo and Hong Kong and challenges them for the title of the cultural and economic capital of the Far East; yet at the same time it looks toward Los Angeles, Chicago and other American cities, which it hopes to outdo with growth rates and a development pattern that are unequalled in history. Shanghai is speeding toward a future that is already happening, just like its magnetic levitation train that quickly covers the 20 miles (32 km) that join the city's center to the new airport in Pudong, whizzing along at 285 mph (460 km/h).

For a western journalist, Shanghai is the biggest professional frustration there is, because as one writes the city is already changing: blueprints are already works in progress; works in progress are already finished. In a city where building sites work for 24 hours a day, 365 days a year, and where millions of immigrants arrive from the countryside to gather the fruits of the economic boom, ideas become reality in the blink of an eye. Just ten years ago, bicycles in their millions were the main mode of transport in the city, so much so that there were special one-way roads for them. At that time, Pudong was a plain of hovels and swamps between the Huangpu river and the East China Sea. Who would have thought that it would become the greatest expanse of skyscrapers in the world, that its traffic would be revolutionized by tens of thousands of taxis (with a taximeter that automatically issues receipts in Chinese and English), by tunnels passing under the river, by futuristic bridges and tangles of motorway viaducts that can only be compared to those around Los Angeles airport?

The city has sought to curb the traffic and keep it under control by introducing a limited number of car registrations: only 6000 a month, with astronomical road tax. What is more, Shanghai is far from being a cheap city: the average income is somewhere near that of southern Europe, and is twelve times higher than that in China's more backward rural areas, but rents are very high and property prices rival those in Tokyo, making prices in Europe and America seem laughable by comparison.

Shanghai is considered the last, and most profitable, frontier of luxury and fashion. All the Italian, French, American and Japanese fashion designers have opened emporiums and boutiques there. Mercedes and BMWs have now become the order of the day and in 2004 a Formula One track was opened, with fourteen curves and two straight stretches bordered by replicas of watchtowers. Cosmopolitan and sophisticated, Shanghai is chic, thanks to its five-star hotel chains if nothing else, which proliferate with their science fiction-style designs among the 4.8 million sq. yards (4 million sq. m) covered by skyscrapers in Pudong. Many of the deals that bring wealth and prestige to the city are struck in the panoramic bar on the 87th floor of the Grand Hyatt and in other large hotels. Shanghai is currently the city that attracts the most foreign investments, capital which comes mainly from "overseas Chinese" as the locals call them here; the diaspora of 60 million emigrants who made their fortunes in South East Asia, in Europe, American and Australia, and who now see China – their mother country – as the most lucrative deal going.

Shanghai is China's undisputed cultural capital and an important market for contemporary art. It produces books and artifacts that leave many Chinese perplexed, such as the novels of its most famous female writers, translated for sale the world over: the angry and unscrupulous Wei Hui of *Shanghai Baby* and Mian Mian of *Lalala*. These young women tell stories that upset Chinese morality and the patriotic vocation to always work as a team; they depict the uncomfortable image of Shanghai as a place of ill-repute, very similar to how westerners saw it in the late 19th and early 20th centuries. After the Communist triumph, Mao Zedong defined the city as "the prostitute of Asia," because its model of development and its humiliating deference to European powers were a source of shame for the whole of China. It was certainly a lively intellectual hub, but at the same time it was one big market. Since China's defeat in the first Opium War (1839-1842), Shanghai had become the corrupt, debauched nerve center of foreign trading concessions; it was one of the cruelest theaters of western imperialism, a city of merciless inequality and widespread vice, with an urban proletariat that was so poor and subjugated that there lives were reminiscent of slavery. Inside the concessions, Chinese workers were ghettoized in the *longtang*, walled-in areas with gates that were closed at night. It is no coincidence that in 1921, the founding congress of the Chinese Communist Party was held here. When the revolution triumphed in 1949, Mao brought the city back under the constraints of a Chinese code of ethics, as well as a Communist one.

The western image of Shanghai at that time was entirely different. The city was seen as sophisticated and romantic, idealized in a mystified imaginary geography of pleasure and peopled by romantic dolls, like the one played by Rita Hayworth in the 1947 film *The Lady from Shanghai*, directed by Orson

Welles. That unmistakeable atmosphere, mingling the colonial and the exotic, can still be felt along the Bund. The Neo-Gothic, Victorian, Art Nouveau and Art Déco shops that lined it are still intact, like a historic and aesthetic rival attraction to the towers and skyscrapers of Pudong, on the opposite bank of a river that is always filled with boats. In a city that is otherwise ruled by modernity, one of the few remaining old-fashioned sights is from that fabulous era: the Neo-Gothic Peace Hotel (formerly the Hotel Cathay, built in the 1920s). It still hosts the nostalgic little concerts of the Old Jazz Band, a group of elderly men who have been playing since time immemorial. Here

in 1932 the director Josef von Sternberg set the film *Shanghai Express*, starring Marlene Dietrich; she used to say that, east of the Suez, only in Shanghai could one buy a decent hat.

A Chinese Shanghai remains as testimony to that era: the old city, a labyrinth of alleyways that is now full of festoons and red lanterns, a maze of shops selling cloth, costume jewellery, souvenirs and tasty titbits among the incense smoke, spring songs, and the smells of food and noodles tossed in the air by cooks who seem like jugglers. This is where the Yu Yuan is to be found: the garden of the mandarin Yu, where nature has been modeled to reproduce a typical southern landscape, evoking woods, lakes, rivers and mountains. Inside the market named after the garden, the Yuyuan Shangchang, is the oldest teahouse in Shanghai; it is housed in the Huxinting, a pavilion at the center of an artificial network of ponds and canals and reached by crossing over a traditional zigzag bridge. But this is no longer a city for tourists; the true Shanghai is the one that, in the words of China's modernizer Deng Xiaoping, "must become the socialist Hong Kong in order to galvanize the whole country." That target has been reached and surpassed, far beyond the most optimistic forecasts of the eminent Deng. (M.M.)

166–167 TODAY'S SHANGHAI HAS A SCI-FI LOOK WITH THE ORIENTAL EAST PEARL TV & RADIO TOWER, THE CEMENT COMMUNICATIONS TOWER THAT IS 468 METRES HIGH, AND THE BARCELO CONGRESS CENTRE, WITH ITS AUDITORIUM ENCLOSED IN A HUGE GLASS BUBBLE.

168 LIKE A BAMBOO CANE OR A SILVERY PAGODA THE JINMAO, IN THE PUDONG AREA, RISES OVER EIGHTY-EIGHT FLOORS, THROWING THE CITY'S CHALLENGE FOR UNPRECEDENTED ECONOMIC GROWTH TOWARDS THE SKY.

168-169 THIS PHOTOGRAPH SHOWS IN THE INTERIOR OF THE GRAND HYATT HOTEL IN PUDONG, SHANGHAI, IN THE JINMAO TOWER. ITS PANORAMIC BAR ON THE EIGHTY-SEVENTH FLOOR IS THE SETTING FOR MANY NEW BUSINESS DEALS IN THE CITY WHICH IS CURRENTLY ATTRACTING THE MOST FOREIGN INVESTMENTS.

170-171 THE MODERN SCULPTURE SHOWN HERE IS DEDICATED TO THE BEIJING 2008 OLYMPIC GAMES, THE FIRST OLYMPICS TO BE HELD IN CHINA; THEY HAVE PROVIDED THE MOTIVATION FOR A RADICAL OVERHAUL OF THE CAPITAL'S URBAN LANDSCAPE.

172-173 THE CARRIAGE OF AN OLD RICKSHAW IS PULLED ALONG BY A MOTOR SCOOTER, AN IMAGE THAT SYMBOLISES THE GREAT CHANGES THAT ARE UNDERWAY IN CHINA, WHERE THE PAST AND THE FUTURE MINGLE IN THE DAILY LIFE OF ITS INHABITANTS.

174-175 THE SUN RISES ABOVE THE FUTURISTIC PUDONG SKYLINE. WHAT USED TO BE A MARSH FULL OF HOVELS AT THE END OF THE EIGHTIES IS NOW WHERE MORE SKYSCRAPERS ARE BUILT THAN ANYWHERE ELSE IN THE WORLD.

176-177 SHANGHAI'S NIGHT TIME ILLUMINATION WITH THE PHOSPHORESCENT COLOURS OF THE MOTORWAY NETWORK GIVES THE CITY AN EVER-MORE FUTURISTIC APPEARANCE: MANY OBSERVERS ARE CONVINCED THAT THIS IS THE CITY IN WHICH CHINA'S FUTURE WILL BE PLAYED OUT.

178-179 AS THIS IMAGE SHOWS, IN SEVERAL AREAS OF SHANGHAI PEDESTRIANS ARE ENTERTAINED BY GIGANTIC VIDEOS THAT ALTERNATE SHOWS WITH ADVERTISING AND PUBLIC INFORMATION NOTICES.

180 A junk glides by in front of the futuristic Hong Kong skyline: the past and present of a city that is full of contradictions.

181 These pictures show three different aspects of the city: the New International Airport in Chek Lap Kok, Queensway with its skyscrapers and a shopping mall glittering with neon lights.

HONG KONG

THE PORT OF CHINA

Seen from Victoria Peak, the glittering lights around the bay of Hong Kong can only be compared to those of Manhattan. The richest city in China and one of the wealthiest on earth, it boasts the highest concentration of Mercedes and Rolls-Royces, an infinity of luxury hotels, the third highest per-capita income in the world after the United States and Japan, and record-breaking gold and monetary reserves per inhabitant. It is one of the main ports, manufacturing and financial centers of the Far East. The first industrial concern began activity in Hong Kong in 1843, but it was only in the 1960s that the city established itself as a manufacturing center. Its businesses have kept their administrative headquarters here, but around a decade ago they transferred their factories, which employ over 5 million people, to the Shenzhen region, just beyond what until a few years ago was the border with the People's Republic. So when the British flag was lowered on July 1, 1997 Hong Kong was already economically integrated with China. Apart from the industrial synergy, the majority of the Asian giant's exports were loaded in Hong Kong harbor. The annexing to China took place with a special statute that granted Hong Kong political and economic autonomy, a free press, its own currency and a different passport for a period of fifty years. In what is considered one of the four most beautiful bay cities (together with Rio de Janeiro, San Francisco and Sydney), the greatest change after 1997 was the obligatory study in schools of *putonghua*, the official language of the People's Republic, to the detriment of English and Cantonese.

Hong Kong is the most futuristic metropolis, with its forest of skyscrapers that soar upward with pointed, squared, elliptical shapes, that tower above with black, blue, golden window panes. After sundown, these straight walls of glass are colored by animated designs and bright advertising hoardings. Steel and cement buildings, built with bamboo scaffolding: the plant that symbolizes oriental tenacity is now used in western-style town planning. An even more futuristic element of the city is the road plan of Hong Kong island, the original nucleus of the former British colony: 32 sq. miles (80 sq. km) of barren land ceded to Britain by China in 1841, after its defeat in the first Opium War. Pedestrian thoroughfares and car lanes are built at different levels; the ground level is reserved for car and double-decker tram traffic, which rages 24 hours a day, forking out over the cement intersections. Human beings, therefore, walk along pavements and viaducts attached to the first floors of the buildings: a labyrinth of paths, squares and raised walkways leading to banks, hotels and shopping centers. Hollywood Road, the antiques dealers' street, leads to Shelley Street via an escalator that rises for almost a mile through the hillside district of Soho.

Hong Kong's creative soul is to be found in Wanchai, in the heart of the old British colony. This is the area that produces directors who, making films in disused factories, win public and critical acclaim at European film festivals. It was from here, in the Seventies, that the Bruce Lee phenomenon transformed the ancient art of *gungfu* into a million-dollar business. Here, Chinese nouvelle cuisine is experimented with, and art galleries have their premises. The intellectual elite meets at the China Club. Central Avenue, the area's main thoroughfare, is studded with the world's most famous designer boutiques. And then there is the emporium of Shanghai Tang, Hong Kong's most successful fashion designer, who is lauded by fashion magazines and has a boutique in New York.

Hong Kong is a golden world, or would be were it not for the dusty back streets that, behind the shining façades of the avenues, have peeling walls, dripping air conditioners, crowded balconies and people sleeping everywhere.

These contrasts and swarms of people, like something out of *Blade Runner*, tell of a city that has an average density of over 6000 people per sq. km, but in central areas can reach ten times that number. It was in fact Kowloon, the 19 sq. mile (47 sq. km) peninsular that Britain seized from China in 1860, where in 1982 Ridley Scott directed some of his film's most remarkable scenes – such as the one in which the low-flying jet passes over a street scattered with open-air restaurants and food cooking in woks and over open fires. The street with its hundreds of tables still exists, and is one of the best places to go for dinner. However, the scene could never be repeated, because in 1998 the old airport in the city center made way for the futuristic hub of Chek Lap Kok; it is the largest airport in Asia with an annual capacity of 35 million passengers. The terminal is the work of the British architect Sir Norman Foster, who also designed the Hong Kong and Shanghai Bank building; it has glass walls and roofs in order to make the most of the sunlight. It is built on an artificial island which was obtained by levelling two rocky cliffs, and is linked to the city center by a train that travels at 85 mph (135 km/h), as well as motorways and a heliport with flights to Wanchai. Chek Lap Kok has turned Hong Kong into the main logistical center of the Far East; this is also home to Cathay Pacific, the Hong Kong airline, which was set up in 1946 and is considered one of the best in the world for the quality of its service.

According to *fengshui*, the Chinese geomantic theory used to determine the correct location of buildings, the new airport will be the key to the city's success. In Hong Kong, ancient Chinese beliefs mix with business and high technology: in the Confucian temple of Won Tai Sin, managers burn incense, offer food to the gods and consult the oracles, all the while taking calls on their cell phones. Fortune-tellers are asked how to win, either on the stock exchange or at the racetrack at Happy Valley: it is the only hope that the middle classes have of acquiring the astronomical amounts needed to buy an apartment. "The most important thing here is money, in part because social security and welfare do not exist," says Koon Lung, the *fengshui* consultant who worked on Sir Norman Foster's Hong Kong Bank building. "The two lions at the entrance represent strength and the universal opposed and complementary principles of *yin* and *yang*. The inside of the building is empty, to receive the energy transmitted by sunlight. The oblique escalator is in the right direction for bringing money to the first floor where the bank counters are. The bank has two doors, one facing the mountain where the money comes from, the other facing the sea, which is a source of positive influences," Koon Lung explains, with a language and appearance that make him seem more of a businessman than a sage.

In its new relationship with China, ultra-modern Hong Kong also acts as a treasure box of memories, as it has kept traditional customs which have long been neglected elsewhere, from *fengshui* to Confucian rites, from gastronomy to *gungfu*, which was made popular again all over the world by Bruce Lee's films. While in Beijing in the 1960s the Cultural Revolution attempted to eradicate every ancient tradition, Hong Kong was importing not only people but also knowledge, customs, rites and even recipes from all over the provinces. In the early Nineties, this knowledge was transposed to annual gastronomic events that, through a galaxy of restaurants, offer a panorama over all the regional cuisines of the most prolific and creative culinary tradition in the world: this is yet another way to get to know a side of China that was at risk of disappearing. (M.M.)

186-187 This image shows Dardin Hous and Exchange Square Towers, which are some of the most modern skyscrapers in Hong Kong, the futuristic city where the director Ridley Scott filmed *Blade Runner*.

188-189 One of the numerous double-decker trams that move through the congested streets of Wanchai, the central commercial area. Hong Kong is the only city in the world with this form of transport.

190 A man shops at the bird market. Keeping caged songbirds is a passion all over China, from the countryside to the most futuristic cities such as Shanghai and Hong Kong.

191 A corner of old China survives in the streets of this frenetic city, in the tired eyes of an elderly woman wearing a traditional hat.

192-193 HUNDREDS OF BELIEVERS CROWD TOGETHER TO LIGHT INCENSE FOR THE GODS IN THE TEMPLE OF WONG TAI SIN IN KOWLOON, TO CELEBRATE NEW YEAR, WHICH IS THE MOST IMPORTANT FESTIVAL IN THE CHINESE LUNAR CALENDAR.

194-195 Hong Kong's
architectural oddities include
The Whanpoa, a shopping centre
in the shape of a ship, built among
the apartment blocks of the
Hung Hom area. It contains
shops, restaurants and cinemas.

196-197 This night-time image
shows the futuristic allure of
the skyscrapers of Hong Kong,
which is one of the most modern
cities in the world, its nights
galvanized by millions of neon
signs in every possible colour.

198-199 This photo shows the main artery of Kowloon, a shopping street with thousands of shops selling all sorts of goods, but above all technological products. The night is lit up by a multitude of neon signs.

199 This image of Kowloon's shopping street lit up by the neon shop signs. Here there are boutiques, jewellers' and high-tech emporiums that stay open late into the night.

200 AND 200-201 As we can see in these two pictures, a night in Hong Kong never stops: together with shopping, the entertainment continues with night clubs, restaurants and all sorts of shows in all areas of the city.

THE DRAGON'S CHILDREN

202 CLOCKWISE FROM LEFT AND 203 Children in action; an actor putting on his make-up; Chinese New Year celebrations; preparing noodles; setting up a huge dragon for the Festival of Lanterns in the square.

204 AND 205 FROM LEFT TO RIGHT Group of Miaio women; preparing a huge red lantern to celebrate Chinese New Year; a man lays out bread to be steamed.

THE DRAGON'S CHILDREN

In China, the economic boom and the race toward modernity live side by side with the country's search for its roots in tradition. This is because the new challenge of globalization also involves getting back to the cultural values of the past. The government itself tends to offer incentives for activities that could contribute to a rediscovery of the sense of national identity. For several years it has been reopening temples and restoring monuments built during the various imperial dynasties. All over the country, interest is growing in all those aspects of ancient Chinese wisdom that were partly denied or completely repressed in the Maoist utopia, especially during the frenzied years of the Cultural Revolution. People are rediscovering martial arts, especially *gongfu* (often transliterated as kung-fu) and *taiji* (tai-chi), traditional medicine, geomancy, music, theater, dance, calligraphy (a supreme discipline), gastronomy (eating is considered the best recreation) and the art of gardens, to mention but a few. They are also returning to traditional festivals and rites that express popular spirituality, solemn ceremonies celebrated spectacularly such as the Feast of Lanterns and those dedicated to the moon and the dead. Paramount, however, is New Year, when the Chinese invoke good fortune with parades of paper dragons, with prayers, red lanterns, fireworks and incense burned in honor of their forebears. The dates of these popular festivals are set on the basis of the age-old calendars that have been in use in China since the country's origins and which are dedicated to the two cosmic elements that divide time: the Sun and the Moon.

It is always difficult to sum up the various 'souls' of this immense country which, in addition to the Han majority, is inhabited by fifty-six ethnic minorities each of which has its own heritage of values, languages, cuisines and costumes. However, festivals and traditions often derive from archaic practices and cults associated with the peasant world, with that rural context in which both Confucianism and Taoism have their roots; these complementary philosophies of the same culture have deeply influenced the history and lifestyle of the Chinese people. Confucianism has ruled society, politics, family life and learning. Taoism places the emphasis on harmony between people and nature, the search

for equilibrium through art, physical well-being, divination and balance between opposite elements, such as the concept of *yin* and *yang* (the female and male elements) underlying Chinese thought. These two schools of thought were later joined by Buddhism, which reached China from India and Central Asia in the first few centuries A.D. Such beliefs and traditions could seem to be at odds with the pragmatism and futuristic dynamism of Beijing. However, they do in fact form the basis of the knowledge and ethics of a country in which skyscrapers are built with scaffolding made from bamboo, the plant that symbolizes the strength and tenacity of the Orient – where, on the strength of four thousand years of history, the future is being built. (M.M.)

206 At New Year the streets fill up with festive processions and colourful paper dragons.

207 TOP LEFT The sound of tambourines accompanies the New Year celebrations.

THE TIME
OF THE SUN AND MOON

As part of this return to ancient customs, many festivities celebrated over the centuries have been reassessed; previously they had been neglected for some time; they had been passed down from a world that was intended to be eradicated, and were reminders of China's imperial past. As noted earlier, the dates of popular festivities are set on the basis of the historic calendar. The two elements that determine how time is divided are the Sun and the Moon, governing the solar and lunar calendars respectively. Both have been used in China since its earliest days. While the Gregorian calendar imported from the West is now commonly used, even today the old "lunar-solar" calendar is still used in rural areas. Instead of having 12 months, the solar calendar is divided up into 24 periods (*jieqi*) of 15 days each. In addition, the years are calculated in sexagesimal cycles (cycles lasting sixty years). Every cycle is then divided into five series of twelve years, each of which is represented by one of the twelve animals in the Taoist zodiac: rat, ox, tiger, hare, dragon, snake, horse, goat, monkey, rooster, dog and boar or pig. So for the Chinese, human destiny and character are determined by the year of birth and not the month. This differs from Western astrology, with its emphasis on the month of birth.

The most important time of year is New Year, which falls between January and February and is also called the Festival of Spring (*chunjie*) because it coincides with the plowing- and sowing-time. In the past, it celebrated the renewal of the spirit in harmony with the reawakening of nature: just when the earth is at its most fertile and the trees are covered with blossoms, a new beginning is also celebrated in the life of the individual. During these days, the family comes together and visits relatives, friends and acquaintances to exchange good wishes. For the occasion, the Chinese clean their houses and decorate them with festoons, red lanterns and flowers. Even nowadays, the windows of shops and houses are hung with long strips of red paper with greetings on them, which wish for luck and success in business, happiness, long life and many children, or, in the countryside, a plentiful harvest. Red is in fact the color of happiness and

207 TOP RIGHT A group of girls salutes the New Year by beating huge drums.

207 BOTTOM An ancient building in Nanjing on the banks of the river Huai is lit up for a festival.

209 TOP PEOPLE OF ALL GENERATIONS REGULARLY PRACTISE MARTIAL ARTS AT DAWN. IN THIS PHOTO, CHILDREN PRACTISE GONGFU IN THE YUYUAN SHANGCHANG, IN THE OLD CITY OF SHANGHAI. THE ANCIENT TEAHOUSE CAN BE SEEN IN THE BACKGROUND.

209 BOTTOM *GONGFU* HAS HAD A NEW SURGE IN POPULARITY ALL OVER CHINA SINCE THE 1990S. THE SHAOLIN MONASTERY IN THE HENAN PROVINCE, WHERE THIS MARTIAL ART WAS INVENTED, IS ONE OF THE MOST POPULAR DOMESTIC TOURIST DESTINATIONS.

joy, as well as marriage. New Year is celebrated with succulent banquets – particularly in the north, these include dumplings, symbolizing abundance and prosperity – and by letting off bangers or fireworks, which are believed to keep evil spirits away. Multicolored paper dragons slither through the streets and squares of cities and villages, held up by long trains of people who can be made out by their legs only.

The 15th day of the 1st lunar month is the turn of the Festival of Lanterns (*yuanxiaojie*), with nocturnal parades with colored paper lanterns creating dreamlike scenes: the round ones can be rolled on the ground like balls of fire, while animal-shaped lanterns (horses or roosters, for example) are moved along on wheels. There are also rectangular-shaped lanterns, some of which conceal internal mechanisms, while others are punched so as to project lucky characters outward. During these feasts every family eats *yuanxiao*, stuffed rice balls that symbolize unity and family harmony. Meanwhile, in the streets shows derided under communism but that have come back into fashion recently take place: one of the best loved is the lion dance, which originated from ancient exorcist practices. One dancer moves the wooden head while another moves the back part of the mythological animal, which acts as guardian and protector against demons.

In early April, on the 12th day of the 3rd lunar month, is the Feast of Qingming, the day of the dead, when incense and false banknotes are burned in honor of the ancestors.

On the 5th day of the 5th lunar month, the Feast of the Dragon Boats (*duanwujie*) is celebrated. During this day, large teams of rowers challenge each other on boats with sterns resembling monstrous creatures. In September, on the 15th day of the 8th lunar month, another important day is celebrated, the Feast of Mid Autumn (*zhongqiujie*) or of the Moon, which is an important time for families to get together. A food typically eaten at this festival is the traditional *yuebing*, a small cake in the shape of a moon.

And so, after the breeze of pragmatism that communism brought with it, China is turning back to Asia, where an element of magic is to be found in all aspects of life. The high technology that, together with hard work, is the secret of this country's phenomenal growth, is still mixed with superstition. Fortune-tellers thrive: divination, after all, is one of the foundations of Taoism. Fate is not tempted and important actions are not carried out at unfavorable times, and clothes of the wrong color are not worn on special occasions. People do not hold weddings on days that are not recommended by numerology, and do not get married in grey, black or blue. These are unlucky colors, unlike red, white and yellow, which bring good luck. All over the country, before anyone builds a house he or she will consult with a *fengshui* expert. *Fengshui* (meaning "wind and water") is the geomantic theory whereby the location and construction of a building must reflect the harmony and order of the universe. Several factors contribute to this balance, such as the arrangement relating to the north-south axis. The entrance should always be south-facing, as negative forces could come in from the north. Other rules make it possible to identify the best relationship with the surrounding water, trees and rocks.

Martial arts, especially *gongfu* play a crucial role in this return to tradition. This discipline is widespread and is made up of two main styles that complement each other: the "external" style (*Shaolinquan*), and the "internal" one (*taijiquan*). *Taiji* is a discipline based on the circulation of vital energy (*qi*). It involves breathing exercise and gymnastics to guide and harmonize energy and integrate mind and body, strengthening the limbs and internal organs. *Taiji* combines rapid movements with slower ones in order to alternate *yin* and *yang*, the opposite principles that make up the world: the compensation of male and female, strength and relaxation, Earth and Heaven. It is a discipline that can be practiced by all, even the elderly: in every city, at dawn, there are groups of old people creating fantastic figures in the greenery of the parks. The province that symbolizes martial arts is Henan. In the county of Wen is the village of Chenjiagou, where it is thought that *taiji* originated, while around 43 miles (70 km) from the capital Zhengzhou stands Songshan; this is one of the sacred mountains of Taoism, on the top of which is the Shaolin monastery, the cradle of *gongfu*. (M.M.)

210 Shows with coloured paper dragons are still the mainstay of Chinese New Year celebrations. Dragons that are many metres long are made to snake through the streets by tens of men moving them with sticks.

210-211 The triumph of colours and movement in this picture gives an idea of how important New Year celebrations are in China, where traditional rites and customs are being rediscovered in parallel with the economic boom.

212-213 The photograph of this woman in costume, holding a lantern, was taken during a parade through the streets of the southern city of Shenzhen; the style and costumes are inspired by style of the Peking Opera.

214-215 To celebrate Chinese New Year, this boy does a dance in which the fluttering of the flags is combined with the sound of tambourines.

215 A very long paper dragon dances through Nanjinglu, the most famous shopping street in Shanghai, to celebrate Chinese New Year.

216-217 A GROUP OF GIRLS CELEBRATES CHINESE
NEW YEAR WITH THE FAN DANCE, AN ANCIENT
CHOREOGRAPHIC DISCIPLINE THAT IS ENJOYING
NEW-FOUND POPULARITY ALL OVER CHINA. AT
DAWN, WOMEN ALSO PERFORM THE DANCE ON THE
BUND IN SHANGHAI.

218-219 A PERFORMER IS AT WORK AMONG THE
VAST FANTASTIC CREATURES' HEADS MADE OF
PAPIER MACHÉ FOR CHINESE NEW YEAR
CELEBRATIONS.

220-221 The beginning of the lunar calendar is a pretext for the most imaginative creations, such as this giant fish which is a New Year's decoration in the Yuyuan in Shanghai.

221 This image of a street in Shanghai gives an idea of the explosion of light and colour with which the Chinese see in the New Year.

222-223 Another colossal dragon celebrates Chinese New Year: sometimes hundreds of craftspeople work on the construction of these immense "costumes".

224 TOP Cooking in the wok and steaming in bamboo baskets are among the most common methods in Chinese cuisine.

224 BOTTOM AND 225 FROM LEFT TO RIGHT The Chinese often eat in the open air and roast ducks are sold in the streets, as are fried snacks and steamed corn on the cob.

CHOPSTICKS
AT THE READY

The Chinese are fascinated by the strength and discipline of the Shaolin monks, but less enthusiastic about their diet, as they consider eating as the greatest pleasure possible. While Mao asserted that "the revolution is not a gala dinner," and transformed the cuisine with the most recipes in the world into a proletarian canteen, in today's China the rediscovery of gastronomy is a key aspect. After the Communist victory in 1949, the Great Helmsman addressed his most arduous task: to feed the most populous country in the world, which was afflicted by decades of famines. Today, however, to the tapping of chopsticks, thousands of regional recipes have been rediscovered, having been lost as a result of wars and revolutions. In recent years, 3.5 million restaurants have opened, employing 68 million people. Each province has a different culinary tradition. The four main types of cooking (one for each cardinal point of the compass) are those of Peking (now Beijing), Canton, Shanghai, and Sichuan. Peking cuisine, which is fairly refined, is the heir to the imperial tradition and is just the feather in the cap of the varied panorama of cuisines in the northern regions, as far north as Mongolia. In addition to beef and pork, in these areas lamb and sometimes mutton are also eaten. Dough in its various forms is also common: dumplings and steamed bread, thick and fine noodles. The most famous speciality of Peking's cuisine is undoubtedly glazed duck, an extremely sophisticated dish, in great part due to the elegant way in which it is presented. The cuisine if Canton is the most omnivorous and is the best known in the West; people in other areas of China say "The Cantonese will eat anything that flies except aeroplanes, anything in the water except boats, and anything with legs except tables." It uses various cooking method, from steaming to baking *en croûte* and frying. The tradition of the east, which has Shanghai as its epicenter, stands out for its fish and seafood and the art of cutting vegetables in the shape of flowers, birds and dragons. This tradition was important from the coastal regions of southern China. Here are lotus leaves, which give off a delicate aroma that adds a touch of refined exoticism to some dishes. The cuisine of Sichuan, in the west, prefers stronger flavors and spicier foods. It uses a variety of spices including chili, black pepper, ginger and coriander to flavor meat and fish that is cooked, marinated or smoked. In China, what one eats is important, but so is how one eats. The *xiuxi*, the two-hour lunch break, is sacred. In order to enjoy lunch in the best way, the perfect number of guests around the table is eight. All the mandatory dishes are then ordered, with cold starters, fried main courses, sweet dishes, followed by spicy ones, accompanied by a hot aromatic soup to help digest it all, and finally dessert, consisting of fruit and sweets. For the Chinese, eating is the best way to stay in shape. Before prescribing medicines, doctors give patients a diet to follow as their health depends in part on various ingredients in food and ways of consuming meals and drinks. The Chinese eat everything, meat and fish, but especially vegetables, and are not fond of dairy products. An infinite variety of leafy green vegetables make up the main part of the meal; to this, a little meat or fish is added, and rice or noodles, all of which is often seasoned with generous doses of aromatic herbs. The great panacea is green tea, which the Chinese drink at all hours and in vast quantities. References to China's rich and varied culinary tradition can be found in stories throughout the nation's literature, from classic to modern and contemporary writing. For the Chinese, in addition to being one of the main – and rare – pleasures in life, food should be taken seriously: as it is so closely linked to individual and collective experience, it is an indispensable element of China's cultural heritage. (M.M.)

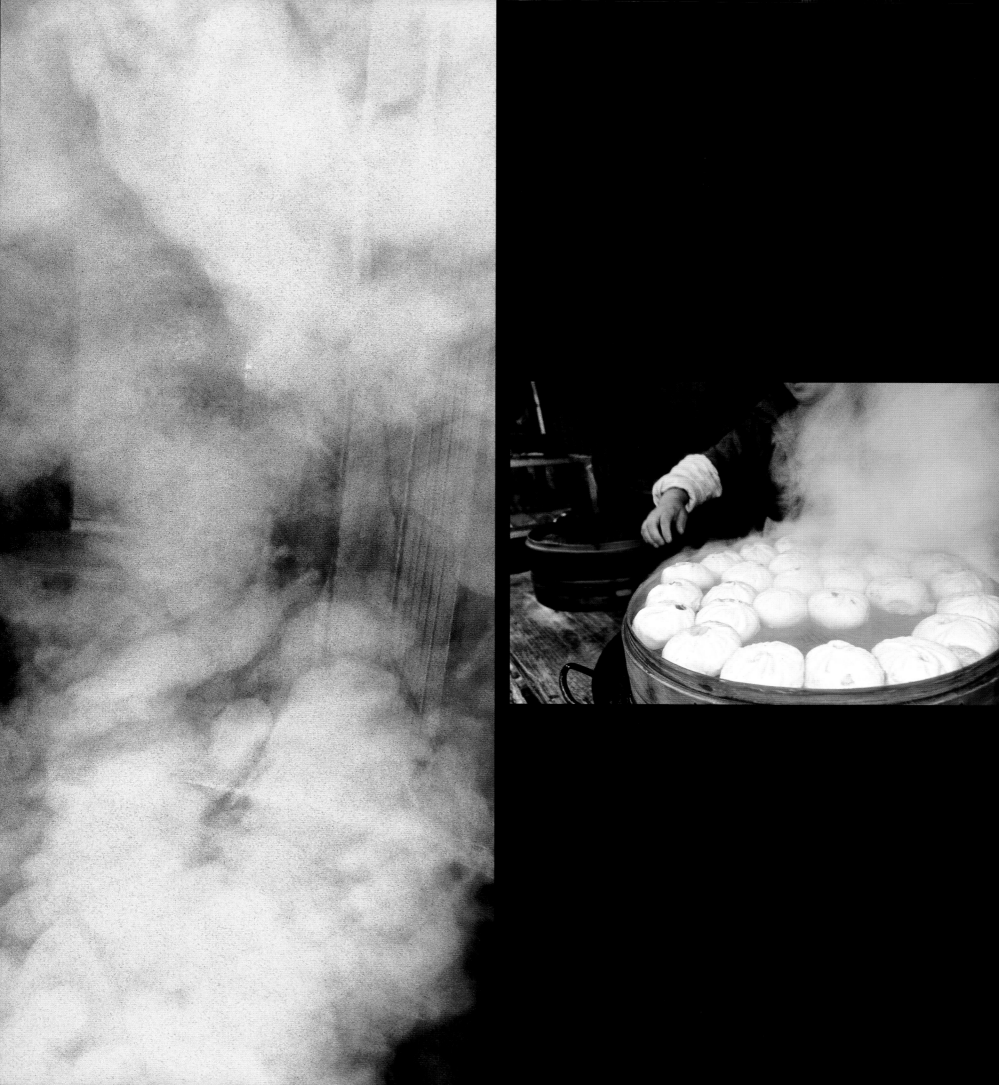

226-227 In Guizhou an elderly man lays out noodles to dry in the sun.

228-229 6-7 Making noodles – from wheat, soya or rice – is an art. Chefs show off their skills in cutting and dividing the strands, like this man in the market at Kashgar in the Xinjiang province.

230-231 AND 231 In these two pictures of Suzhou, women steam a type of bread filled with meat: this is one of the many dim sum, Cantonese appetisers that are found all over southern China.

232-233 With woks and saucepans, this family from the Muslim Hui minority cooks in the street outside a restaurant in the picturesque Muslim quarter of Xi'an.

234 The photo shows an actor in the Peking Opera, which is the most famous form of Chinese theatre and developed in the capital from 1790 onwards.

235 FROM LEFT TO RIGHT As we can see here, make-up plays a fundamental role in the Peking Opera. Actors have their faces totally masked by cosmetics.

STAGE
ILLUSIONS

One of the most evocative ways to approach Chinese culture is to watch a performance at the Peking Opera. In recent decades the *Jingxi*, or "theater of the capital" has rediscovered its classical forms and the rich repertoire of tales, roles and costumes that the Cultural Revolution had discarded to make way for contemporary characters and themes. It is a unique kind of show, with dancing and acrobatics, sumptuous, colorful costumes, singing and fighting scenes, mimicry and certain conventions that are difficult to decipher for those who are unfamiliar with the code. The set is empty, with a backdrop and two entrances at the sides. Just a few elements are needed to illustrate the place of action, which an experienced audience can recognize easily. The actor-dancers fill this space, creating an illusion of reality thanks to their multiform art; with magic gestures they evoke the enchanted scenery in which the action takes place, helped by the musical accompaniment. Very often they express themselves through song, in an unmistakeable style. But the language of the spoken dialogues also has an extraordinary musicality. The pronunciation used is always that of the north, which has encouraged this style to be taken on as the national type of theater. The actor's face becomes almost expressionless beneath the exaggerated make-up with its bright colors and strong lines. This has the function of communicating precise meanings, by expressing and accentuating the moral traits and personality of the various characters, which fall into four main types. This makes them easily identifiable. The colors are extremely symbolic and express the range of emotions and sentiment, from ferocity to loyalty, from arrogance to prudence, from courage to perfidy, from cunning to

wisdom. Weighed down by sumptuous, heavy costumes which are stunningly expressive, some dancers move solemnly in a circle while others, dressed in lighter costumes, throw themselves into incredible acrobatics. In the costumes too, colors indicate roles and social status: yellow, for example, is only worn by members of the imperial family, while red is worn by high-ranking characters.

Other traditions are revisited, sometimes just as tourist attractions. In Xi'an, the provincial capital of Shaanxi, music and dance shows inspired by the Tang era (618-907) gracefully recall the atmosphere of ancient Chang'an, where the Silk Route once passed through and where East and West melded together in a cosmopolitan world.

Shadow theater, which originated in ancient magic/religious ceremonies in northern China, was also banned during the Cultural Revolution; this is because the puppets were considered symbols of retrograde feudal values. Its remote origins date back to about two thousand years ago. The puppets used to be made of paper but they were soon replaced by two-dimensional shapes cut into cow or sheep hides, or sometimes into donkey or horse hides, depending on the area. During the show, the figures' shadows are projected onto a screen, while voices offstage narrate the story or act out the dialogues; this is often accompanied by singing or playing traditional instruments such as the gong. The artists, hidden behind the screen, skillfully manipulate the sticks, and as if by magic the characters come to life, bewitching the audience. Nowadays, these finely made figures, somewhere between theater and the plastic arts, are collected by individuals and museums (M.M. and F.R.)

236-237 THIS ACTOR IN THE PEKING OPERA IS DEEP IN
CONCENTRATION AS HE MAKES UP HIS FACE; IT IS SUCH AN
IMPORTANT PART OF THE OVERALL EFFECT THAT THE
ARTISTS SOMETIMES TAKE HOURS DOING IT.

237 THE MAKE-UP PLAYS A FUNDAMENTAL ROLE IN THE
DRAMATIC PATHOS CREATED IN THE PEKING OPERA.

238 MALE AND FEMALE ROLES ARE VERY STRONGLY
DIFFERENTIATED IN THE PEKING OPERA.

239 AN ACTOR PAINTS HIS FACE; IN THE PEKING OPERA,
THIS PROCEDURE IS JUST AS IMPORTANT AS ACTING
AND SINGING, BECAUSE IT EXPANDS THE DRAMATIC
CAPACITY OF THE ACTORS.

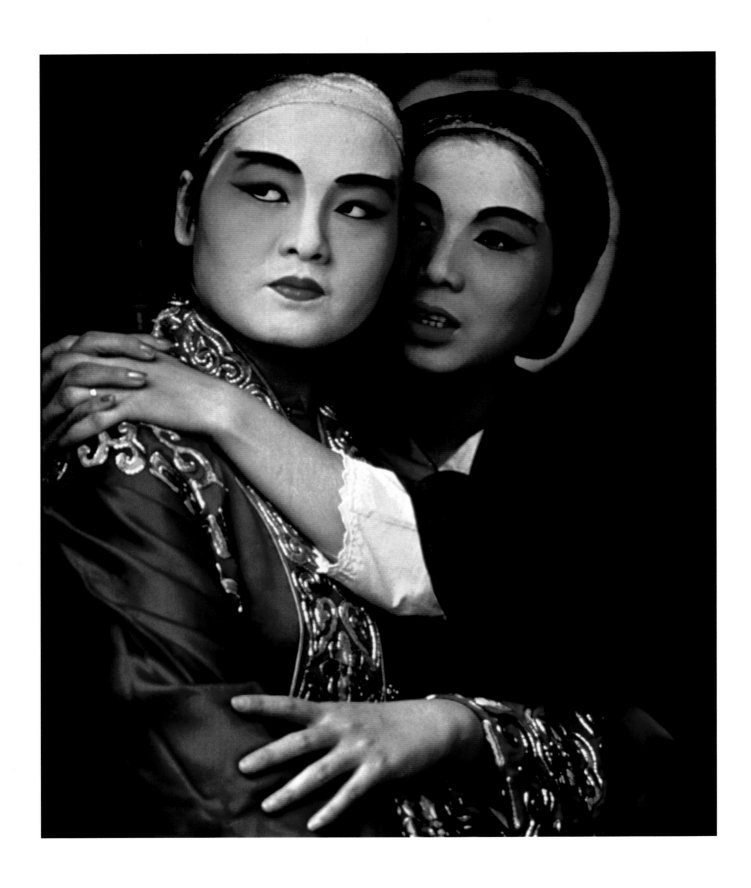

240-241 Actors take part in a theatre/dance show in which make-up, costumes and choreography work together to recreate the historical context in which the scene takes place.

242-243 These two images of actors in the Peking Opera underline how important costumes are in evoking the historical period in which the drama is set.

244-245 This "sleeve dance" is one of the most spectacular moments of the opera "The Legend of the White Snake" *(Baishezhuan)*. It recalls some of the dances of the Tang theatre, which has come back into fashion in the city of Xi'an.

245 This dance, which represents a heavenly fairy scattering flowers, is also based around the movement of the dancer's long sleeves.

246 AND 247 These two spectacular images of the Peking Opera were taken during the China Peking Opera Art Festival in Shanghai, an extraordinary programme of shows that present the best of Chinese theatre tradition.

248-249 AND 249 THE PEKING
OPERA WAS CREATED IN 1790, WHEN
FOUR THEATRE TROUPES ARRIVED IN
THE CAPITAL FROM THE PROVINCE OF
ANHUI, UPON ORDER OF THE
EMPEROR QIANLONG. HERE, IN THE
CENTURIES THAT FOLLOWED, THEY
COMBINED THEIR ART WITH THE
THEATRICAL TRADITION OF HUBEI,
ALSO DRAWING ON THE REPERTOIRE
OF OTHER REGIONAL SCHOOLS SUCH
AS THE KUNQU, THE QINQIANG AND
THE BANGZI.

250-251 In the Peking Opera, the colours of the face make-up represent different roles and personality traits. Yellow and white symbolise cunning, red represents faithfulness and fairness, black stands for value and wisdom, blue and green symbolise vigour and enterprise, while gold and silver denote mysticism and supernatural powers.

252-253 One of the most famous actors of the Peking Opera plays the part of the Monkey (right) in a scene from the drama "Stopping the horse".

253 During the show, this artist in the Peking Opera wears a false beard and an elaborate costume.

AN ETHNIC MOSAIC

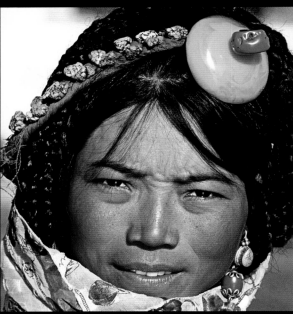

254 CLOCKWISE FROM LEFT A Tibetan woman in Yunnan; Mongolian horseman, Tibetan girl; water-bearer in Guangxi.

255 AND 256 These two women, one holding a lamb and the other with a hairpiece woven from the hair of her ancestors, are from the Miao ethnic group, one of the largest in China.

AN ETHNIC
MOSAIC

Ethnic diversity in China has by now become a cultural resource, and minority groups are at the forefront of the rediscovery of tradition. Over 56 national minorities have been living alongside the dominant ethnic group, the Han, for centuries. Generally, these groups have a specific culture and their own traditional languages; these differ from *putonghua*, the official language of the People's Republic of China.

The Han people are found throughout the country, although they are more concentrated in certain areas, such as the central plain and the areas around the main rivers. The areas in which the minorities are most numerous are most often the outlying regions, among the arid tablelands of the west, the forest-covered mountains in the south and the vast expanses of pasture in the north. Precisely because the minority peoples were situated in border zones that were as strategic as they were desolate, Mao Zedong gave them considerable autonomy and exempted them from the single-child demographic policy, as

well as representing them on the national flag: indeed, one of the many possible interpretations is that the four stars surrounding the large Han star on the red background symbolize the Mongols, the Manchu, the Tibetans and the Muslims in Chinese Turkestan. This tradition probably derives from the meaning of the flag with five stripes that was used in the first years of the Republic, 1912 to 1929.

Although they make up less than 8 percent of the population, ethnic minorities in China have a vast linguistic and religious heritage, with original and truly fascinating customs. The most numerous minority – with over 15 million people – is the Zhuang, which is also one of those that is best integrated with the Han majority. The Zhuang belong to the Thai ethno-linguistic group, and are concentrated in the southwest, in the Guangxi Zhuang Autonomous Region and the nearby provinces of Yunnan, Guangdong, Hunan and Guizhou. The last of these is a region with very rich folklore traditions and which contains over 15 different ethnic groups. The fact that

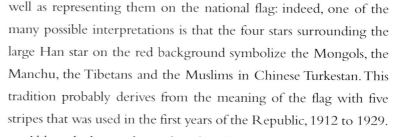

257 TOP LEFT Two Kazakhs go hunting with falcons at the foot of the Tianshan.

257 TOP CENTER The Hakkas are not considered an ethnic minority, but part of the major ethnic group the Han.

257 TOP RIGHT In Shigu, in Yunnan province, a woman carries a curious load on her head.

257 BOTTOM This man from the Miao group wears a beard, which is widespread among the country's fifty-six ethnic minorities.

the Zhuang have their own language, which was only given a written form in the Fifties, was an important factor in the preservation of their identity. Moreover, the Zhuang lifestyle is not very different to that of the Han country people who, like them, work in the paddy fields and the terraced fields of the south. Alongside Buddhism, which is widespread among the Zhuang, traditional cults and beliefs live on, according to which evil spirits control man's destiny. Although they are assimilated, the Zhuang still have some particular customs, for example those related to courting and marriage rites. One of the most important – which was probably passed down from

and are scattered over a fairly large area, especially in Ningxia Hui, Gansu and Qinghai provinces. These areas are the ideal destination for anybody wishing to explore Muslim culture in China, as is Xinjiang. There too, in what used to be the melting pot of peoples along the Silk Route, described by Marco Polo, is Kashgar, the Muslim oasis with earth houses, streets and temples. Here, Turkmen, Kyrgyz, Mongols, Kazakhs and especially Uygurs live; this last is the fifth ethnic group in the country, with over 7 million people. Kashgar is an Arabian Nights-style bazaar, and after the opening-up of trade brought about by Deng Xiaoping, it once again became the center of animated negotiations between men from the desert who wear turbans and travel on Bactrian camels. The Sunday market is attended by over 50,000 people from the 13 ethnic groups living in the surrounding valleys.

The fourth ethnic group in China, and the second largest in the south, is the Miao: also known as the Hmong, there are around 7.5 million of them, and they are mainly found in Hunan,

an ancient matriarchal society – which some people still stick to, is that after the wedding, the groom goes to live with the bride's family and takes his father-in-law's surname.

The Manchu, who founded the Qing dynasty (1644-1912), have now mainly become assimilated, make up the country's second ethnic group, with a population of around 10 million, concentrated in the northeast of China. Next come the Hui, of whom there are more than 8 million; they can be recognized by their typical white skull caps. They make up one of the ten minorities that follow Islam,

Guizhou, Yunnan, Sichuan and Guangxi provinces. Driven by a strongly independent spirit, they have always fought to protect their identity and they live in quite closed communities. Their traditional headdresses and clothes, which are a true kaleidoscope of colors, are a fundamental part of Miao culture, and are among the most spectacular in China. They have a variety of styles that differ, depending on their local tribe; in fact, communities are classified on the basis of the color of their clothing or their hairstyles. The world of the Miao is indeed a flowering of multi-colored clothes, embellished with a pro-

fusion of decorations inspired by the animal and plant world. So there are 'black,' 'red' or 'silver' Miao, depending on the main color they use in their clothing, and then there are Miao with long skirts and those with short skirts, and so on.

Miao headdresses are also a sign of belonging to a certain group. In some areas, girls wear semi-cone-shaped structures with the base turned upward, like crowns, decorated in silver with phoenixes and other birds, flowers, dragons or disks hanging over the forehead. When they move their heads, the ornaments jangle, making a pleasant silvery sound. In another variant, silver strips decorate a pair of ox horns inserted into a tall chignon of hair. Some of the headdresses have specific meanings: for example, one of the male headdresses is made of 10 ft (3 m) of fabric embroidered with floral motifs; one end is left pointing upward to symbolize power. Bird feathers are another form of ornament that is popular among young people, and girls sometimes show off heavy hairdos in the shape of butterflies, made from black wool tied together with white strips.

Craft products among the Miao have the same vivacity and variety, and include splendid fabrics, batik and colorful embroidery. The Miao feast days, sometimes involving horse races and bull fights, often follow the rhythm of the traditional calendar. Singing and dancing, to the sound of the bamboo flute (*lusheng*) and drums is very important for these people.

Another group that is equally well-versed in these disciplines is the Dong, who sing from a very young age. Like the Miao, who live in pretty wooden pile-dwellings, this minority – of which there are around 2.5 million between Hunan, Guangxi and Guizhou provinces – also creates truly unique structures in wood: houses, towers and bridges all have remarkable features, due to the fact that these regions remained isolated for centuries. The Dong also wear their multi-colored traditional costumes for a great number of festivals that they celebrate throughout the year.

The minorities have a great impact in Yunnan, where 25 ethnic groups from 6 different lineages represent over a third of the 43 million inhabitants of this province, which is larger than Germany and stretches from the rainforests of Indochina to the summits of the Himalayas. The minorities in Yunnan are the best example of ethnic diversity and racial, religious and linguistic tolerance to be found in China. This can be seen clearly in Lijiang, the city of the Naxi, a minority which is part of the Tibetan-Burmese ethno-linguistic group. The city's temples, shops and streets are filled with a euphoric music with spring-like notes made by xylophones, drums, gongs, flutes and various stringed instruments. The Naxi women come to the city to shop, with panniers to accommodate their purchases. The children go to school wearing traditional costume, the same as that worn by girls visiting the postcard-pretty bridge and pagoda at the Black Dragon Pond. Or at the market in Shapin, in the Dali valley, where Bai girls from the mountains – another minority from the same lineage – wear tall floral bonnets as they haggle loudly for hens, animal feed, rice, vegetables, baskets, ceramics, fabrics. This is a peasant market, the weekly meeting place for the tribes who live off agriculture and livestock in the surrounding mountains. Among the general activity, barbers shave men, chefs cook noodles, weavers work at their looms, basket makers plait wicker, tobacconists roll cigars and dentists patch together untidy mouths. This small bazaar contains all the color and vitality of Asia.

The most widespread nationality in Yunnan is the Yi. The group belongs to the same ethno-linguistic group as the Naxi and is divided into 40 local subgroups that make up almost 10 percent of the province's population. With over 6.5 million people, the Yi are one of the largest minorities in China, and are also found in the nearby regions of Sichuan, Guizhou and Guangxi provinces. Yi from the Lijiang valley are found in the Stone Forest region, and mountain Yi live on the Jade Dragon range, above the valley: they are yak herders and wear red cloaks with yellow designs and flamboyant marmot-fur caps with long feathers stuck in them.

In this province, in terms of number of people, the Yi are followed by the Bai, Hani, Zhuang, Dai, Miao, Hui (who are Muslims), Lisu, Lahu, Wa, Naxi, Jingpo, Yao and Zang (Tibetans). The other minorities amount to fewer than 100,000 members each. There is such variety that in central Yunnan there is even a fairly large community of Mongols: it is believed that they descended from soldiers who reached these extreme southern regions to conquer the Dali kingdom, which surrendered to the Mongol invaders in 1253.

The Zang, who are Tibetan, live on the Zhongdian tableland. There are over 4.5 million of them throughout China, spread between Tibet, Yunnan, Sichuan, Gansu and Qinghai. The nomads live in tents (*rebo*) and rear yaks, cows and goats. One of the most important clans, which is thought to have extremely pure lineage, is the Khampa; they are skilled horseman and warriors who can be recognized by their typical hairstyle of plaits decorated with threads of red silk. The sedentary clans live in villages clinging to the mountainsides; they cultivate barley and other cereals and carry out craftwork and commerce. Their houses are made from rough earthen bricks or stone, with wooden floors, and are generally two or three stories high. The ground floor is a stall for the animals, while the home is on the upper floors. In summer, the terrace roof functions as a granary. The windows are brightly colored, as are the traditional clothes worn by the Tibetans. This ethnic group is perhaps the furthest from the Han in terms of traditions, and the Tibetans are not used to using chopsticks. Like all the Himalayan peoples, they eat with their hands, and the waiters in their restaurants entertain diners by singing, faithful to ancient traditions. Zang women have premarital sexual freedom and, even after they are married, they are not necessarily expected to be faithful to their husbands. This is an exception in the Far East. Women and children bathe together without embarrassment at the hot springs of the villages. The religion of this ethnic group, which has a strong monastic component, is Lamaism, a specific type of Buddhism which is influenced by Shamanic rites and practices and has a quite complex ritual and ecclesiastic system. As well as in Tibet, Lamaist Buddhism is also widespread in the autonomous region of Inner Mongolia, which is the Chinese province with the greatest number of minorities. Here, in addition to the Han and Mongolian peoples there are forty-seven other ethnic groups; however, in total they only make up 800,000 inhabitants.

The Mongols, who are also found in other areas of China, total almost 5 million overall. They remain faithful to their nomadic lifestyle and ancient traditions, and still live in simple felt tents called *yurte*, on the vast grasslands. They are excellent horsemen, and in addition to riding they also enjoy activities passed down from their intrepid warrior ancestors, such as wrestling or archery. They often challenge each other to spectacular contests that comprise these three disciplines and take place as part of impressive traditional festivals. The most important of these is the *nadamu* ("game" or "fun"), which takes place in summer and lasts for three days. At night, once the competitions are over, the grassland is alight with bonfires, around which young people dance while singing popular songs to the stirring sound of the *matouqin,* the traditional stringed instrument. In Chinese, this name means "horse-head lute," and it is the highest tribute to an animal which is of truly vital importance to this people of shepherds. If it is true that the people of a state can not just be equated with the group that represents the majority, but rather with a composite of all those who live within it, with their individual, varied identities, then China offers a truly unique chance to see an extraordinarily complex and intricate situation. (M.M.)

262-263 THESE TWO MIAO WOMEN,
WITH HAIRSTYLES WOVEN FROM THE
HAIR OF THEIR OWN FOREBEARS,
LAY TOBACCO LEAVES OUT TO DRY
IN THE SUN.

264–265 THIS MIAO WOMAN IS TAKING PART IN A
CULTURAL FESTIVAL IN GUIZHOU PROVINCE. THE MIAO
MINORITY IS FAMOUS FOR THE HIGH QUALITY OF THE
FABRICS EMBROIDERED BY ITS WOMEN.

266–267 A YOUNG MIAO GIRL WEARS A TRADITIONAL
HEADDRESS DURING ONE OF THE MANY FESTIVALS THAT
TAKE PLACE IN THE SOUTHERN PROVINCE OF GUIZHOU.

268-269   THIS OLD LADY CARRYING
A FAGGOT BELONGS TO THE YI ETHNIC
GROUP, WHICH HAS AROUND SIX AND
A HALF MILLION PEOPLE LIVING IN THE
PROVINCES OF SICHUAN, YUNNAN,
GUIZHOU AND GUANGXI.

270-271   THESE TWO CHILDREN IN
TRADITIONAL COSTUMES, SITTING IN
FRONT OF PLAITED CHILLI PEPPERS
LAID OUT TO DRY, BELONG TO ONE OF
THE FORTY SUB-GROUPS OF THE YI
PEOPLE THAT LIVE IN THE YUNNAN
PROVINCE.

272-273   THIS STRIKING HEADDRESS
BELONGS TO A WOMAN OF THE HANI
OR AKHA ETHNIC GROUP, WHICH IS
COMPOSED OF AROUND TWO AND
A HALF MILLION PEOPLE WHO
INHABIT THE AREA COMPRISED
BETWEEN YUNNAN PROVINCE, EASTERN
MYANMAR AND THE NORTHERN PARTS
OF LAOS, VIETNAM AND THAILAND.

274-275   THIS HAKKA WOMAN WEARS
AN UNUSUAL BLACK COSTUME, AND IS
SMOKING TOBACCO IN A TRADITIONAL
OPIUM PIPE (A DRUG WHICH USED TO
BE WIDESPREAD IN THE CELESTIAL
EMPIRE).

276   THESE TWO CHILDREN, PHOTOGRAPHED IN THE
MUSLIM QUARTER OF XI'AN, BELONG TO THE HUI ETHNIC
GROUP, WHICH IS THE RESULT OF THE MIX BETWEEN THE
HAN AND THE MUSLIM CULTURES AT THE TIME WHEN THE
CITY WAS THE EASTERN TERMINUS OF THE SILK ROUTE.

276-277   THE TWO MEN SHOWN HERE IN A STREET
OF KASHGAR BELONG TO THE UYGUR ETHNIC GROUP
(7,200,000 MEMBERS), WHICH HAS TURKISH ORIGINS
AND FOLLOWS ISLAM. THE GROUP LIVES IN THE
NORTH-WESTERN AUTONOMOUS REGION OF XINJIANG.

278-279 THIS MAN LOOKS OUT OF A
SHOP IN KASHGAR, THE MUSLIM CITY
OF XINJIANG, SITUATED AT AN
ALTITUDE OF 1300 METRES ON A
PLATEAU IN THE WESTERN TIP OF
CHINA; IT WAS A CROSSROADS FOR
TURKMENS, KYRGYZS, MONGOLS,
UYGURS AND KAZAKHS ON THE
SILK ROUTE.

280-281 A Kyrgyz woman
performs a funeral rite in her
yurta, a tent that is commonly
found among many peoples of
Turkish and Mongol origins who
live in the mountainous chains
and steppes of Central Asia.

282 A ray of sunlight lights up
the face of a girl from the
Kyrgyz ethnic group, sitting at
home waiting to be called for her
wedding celebration. The Kyrgyzs
remain faithful to rites and
traditions that have remained
unchanged for centuries.

283 This Kyrgyz woman is
preparing a variety of flat
noodles, one of the typical dishes
of this Muslim ethnic group, with
Turkish origins, that lives in the
provinces of Xinjiang and
Heilongjiang, situated at the two
northernmost tips of China.

286 This Kazakh nomad is hunting with an eagle; this is a widespread practice among this ethnic group, which has Mongol origins and was converted to Islam during Turkish expansion.

287 In China, the Kazakhs are a minority, with 1,110,000 members, found in the north-eastern provinces of Xinjiang, Gansu and Qinghai. This group gives its name to the independent state of Kazakhstan (former Soviet Union), situated near the western borders of China.

288-289 THIS WOMAN LYING IN A FIELD WITH HER HORSE IS PART OF THE MONGOLIAN MINORITY, WHICH IS FOUND MAINLY IN INNER MONGOLIA BUT ALSO IN THE PROVINCES OF XINJIANG, LIAONING, JILIN, HEILONGJIANG, GANSU, QINGHAI, HEBEI AND HENAN.

290 AND 291 THE WOMAN ON THE LEFT BELONGS TO THE AMDO SUB-GROUP, WHICH IS PART OF THE TIBETAN ETHNIC GROUP AND COMES FROM A REGION IN THE NORTH-EASTERN PART OF THE AUTONOMOUS PROVINCE OF TIBET. THE TIBETAN MAN ON THE RIGHT BELONGS TO THE KHAMPA SUB-GROUP, A PEOPLE OF HORSEMEN, WARRIORS AND MERCHANTS FROM THE TABLELANDS OF TIBET.

292 AND 293 THESE TIBETAN WOMEN, WHO BELONG TO THE AMDO SUB-GROUP, HAVE DECORATED THEIR HEADS WITH SPECTACULAR HEADDRESS MADE OF CORAL AND TURQUOISE STONES AND BRASS PLATES, TO TAKE PART IN A PILGRIMAGE.

294 AND 295 TIBETAN BUDDHIST MONKS ARE PRAYING AT A TEMPLE. THE MOST FAMOUS LAMAIST BUILDING IS THE POTALA IN LHASA.

INDEX

PHOTOGRAPHIC CREDITS

300 A lone canoe glides along the water on the river Li at Guilin, in Guangxi province.